THE BATTLE
AND THE BREEZE

R. M. BALLANTYNE

1st WORLD
LIBRARY
Literary Society

The Battle and the Breeze

R. M. Ballantyne

© 1st World Library, 2009
PO Box 2211
Fairfield, IA 52556
www.1stworldlibrary.com
First Edition

LCCN: 2009923518

Softcover ISBN: 978-1-4218-8877-4
Hardcover ISBN: 978-1-4218-8976-4
eBook ISBN: 978-1-4218-8778-4

Purchase *"The Battle and the Breeze"*
as a traditional bound book at:
www.1stWorldLibrary.com/purchase.asp?ISBN=978-1-4218-8877-4

1st World Library is a literary, educational organization
dedicated to:

- Creating a free internet library of downloadable ebooks

- Hosting writing competitions and offering book
publishing scholarships.

1st World Library Literary Society

Giving Back to the World

"If you want to work on the core problem, it's early school literacy."

- James Barksdale, former CEO of Netscape

"No skill is more crucial to the future of a child, or to a democratic and prosperous society, than literacy."

- Los Angeles Times

"Literacy... means far more than learning how to read and write... The aim is to transmit... knowledge and promote social participation."

- UNESCO

"Literacy is not a luxury, it is a right and a responsibility. If our world is to meet the challenges of the twenty-first century we must harness the energy and creativity of all our citizens."

- President Bill Clinton

"Parents should be encouraged to read to their children, and teachers should be equipped with all available techniques for teaching literacy, so the varying needs and capacities of individual kids can be taken into account."

- Hugh Mackay

CHAPTER ONE

TOUCHES ON OUR HERO'S EARLY LIFE, EXPERIENCES, AND ADVENTURES

Bill Bowls was the most amiable, gentle, kindly, and modest fellow that ever trod the deck of a man-of-war. He was also one of the most lion-hearted men in the Navy.

When Bill was a baby—a round-faced, large-eyed, fat-legged baby, as unlike to the bronzed, whiskered, strapping seaman who went by the name of "Fighting Bill" as a jackdaw is to a marlinespike—when Bill was a baby, his father used to say he was just cut out for a sailor; and he was right, for the urchin was overflowing with vigour and muscular energy. He was utterly reckless, and very earnest—we might almost say *desperately* earnest. Whatever he undertook to do he did "with a will." He spoke with a will, listened with a will, laughed, yelled, ate, slept, wrought, and fought with a will. In short, he was a splendid little fellow, and therefore, as his father wisely said, was just cut out for a sailor.

Bill seemed to hold the same opinion, for he took to the water quite naturally from the very commencement of life. He laughed with glee when his mother used to put him into the washtub, and howled with rage when she took him out. Dancing bareheaded under heavy rain was his delight, wading in ponds and rivers was his common practice, and tumbling into deep pools was his most ordinary mishap. No wonder, then, that Bill learned at an early age to swim, and also to fear nothing whatever, except a blowing-up from his father. He feared that, but he did not often get it, because, although full of mischief as an egg is full of meat, he was good-humoured and bidable, and, like all lion-hearted fellows, he had little or no malice in him.

He began his professional career very early in life. When in after years he talked to his comrades on this subject, he used to say—

"Yes, mates, I did begin to study navigation w'en I was about two foot high—more or less—an' I tell 'e what it is, there's nothin' like takin' old Father Time by the forelock. I was about four year old when I took my first start in the nautical way; and p'r'aps ye won't believe it, but it's a fact, I launched my first ship myself; owned her; commanded and navigated her, and was wrecked on my first voyage. It happened this way; my father was a mill-wright, he was, and lived near a small lake, where I used to splutter about a good deal. One day I got hold of a big plank, launched it after half an hour o' the hardest work I ever had, got on it with a bit of broken palm for an oar, an' shoved off into deep water. It was a splendid burst! Away I went with my heart in my mouth and my feet in the water tryin' to steady myself, but as ill luck would have it, just as I had got my ship on an even keel an' was beginnin' to dip my oar with great caution, a squall came down the lake, caught me on the starboard quarter, and threw me on my beam-ends. Of coorse I went sowse into the water, and had only time to give out one awful yell when the water shut me up. Fortnitly my father heard me; jumped in and

R. M. Ballantyne

pulled me out, but instead of kicking me or blowin' me up, he told me that I should have kept my weather-eye open an' met the squall head to wind. Then he got hold of the plank and made me try it again, and didn't leave me till I was able to paddle about on that plank almost as well as any Eskimo in his skin canoe. My good old dad finished the lesson by tellin' me to keep always *in shoal water till I could swim,* and to look out for squalls in future! It was lucky for me that I had learned to obey him, for many a time I was capsized after that, when nobody was near me, but bein' always in shoal water, I managed to scramble ashore."

As Bill Bowls began life so he continued it. He went to sea in good earnest when quite a boy and spent his first years in the coasting trade, in which rough service he became a thorough seaman, and was wrecked several times on various parts of our stormy shores. On reaching man's estate he turned a longing eye to foreign lands, and in course of time visited some of the most distant parts of the globe, so that he may be said to have been a great traveller before his whiskers were darker than a lady's eyebrows.

During these voyages, as a matter of course, he experienced great variety of fortune. He had faced the wildest of storms, and bathed in the beams of the brightest sunshine. He was as familiar with wreck as with rations; every species of nautical disaster had befallen him; typhoons, cyclones, and simooms had done their worst to him, but they could not kill him, for Bill bore a sort of charmed life, and invariably turned up again, no matter how many of his shipmates went down. Despite the rough experiences of his career he was as fresh and good-looking a young fellow as one would wish to see.

Before proceeding with the narrative of his life, we shall give just one specimen of his experiences while he was in the merchant service.

Having joined a ship bound for China, he set sail with the proverbial light heart and light pair of breeches, to which we may add light pockets. His heart soon became somewhat heavier when he discovered that his captain was a tyrant, whose chief joy appeared to consist in making other people miserable. Bill Bowls's nature, however was adaptable, so that although his spirits were a little subdued, they were not crushed. He was wont to console himself, and his comrades, with the remark that this state of things couldn't last for ever, that the voyage would come to an end some time or other, and that men should never say die as long as there remained a shot in the locker!

That voyage did come to an end much sooner than he or the tyrannical captain expected!

One evening our hero stood near the binnacle talking to the steersman, a sturdy middle-aged sailor, whose breadth appeared to be nearly equal to his length.

"Tom Riggles," said Bill, somewhat abruptly, "we're goin' to have dirty weather."

"That's so, lad, I'm not goin' to deny it," replied Tom, as he turned the wheel a little to windward:

Most landsmen would have supposed that Bill's remark should have been, "We *have* got dirty weather," for at the time he spoke the good ship was bending down before a stiff breeze, which caused the dark sea to dash over her bulwarks and sweep the decks continually, while thick

R. M. Ballantyne

clouds, the colour of pea-soup, were scudding across the sky; but seafaring men spoke of it as a "capful of wind," and Bill's remark was founded on the fact that, for an hour past, the gale had been increasing, and the appearance of sea and sky was becoming more threatening.

That night the captain stood for hours holding on to the weather-shrouds of the mizzen-mast without uttering a word to any one, except that now and then, at long intervals, he asked the steersman how the ship's head lay. Dark although the sky was, it did not seem so threatening as did the countenance of the man who commanded the vessel.

Already the ship was scudding before the wind, with only the smallest rag of canvas hoisted, yet she rose on the great waves and plunged madly into the hollows between with a violence that almost tore the masts out of her. The chief-mate stood by the wheel assisting the steersman; the crew clustered on the starboard side of the forecastle, casting uneasy glances now at the chaos of foaming water ahead, and then at the face of their captain, which was occasionally seen in the pale light of a stray moonbeam. In ordinary circumstances these men would have smiled at the storm, but they had unusual cause for anxiety at that time, for they knew that the captain was a drunkard, and, from the short experience they had already had of him, they feared that he was not capable of managing the ship.

"Had we not better keep her a point more to the south'ard, sir?" said the mate to the captain, respectfully touching his cap; "reefs are said to be numerous here about."

"No, Mister Wilson," answered the captain, with the gruff air of a man who assumes and asserts that he knows what he is about, and does not want advice.

"Keep her a point to the west," he added, turning to the steersman.

There was a cry at that moment—a cry such as might have chilled the blood in the stoutest heart—

"Rocks ahead!"

"Port! port! hard-a-port!" shouted the men. Their hoarse voices rose above the gale, but not above the terrible roar of the surf, which now mingled with the din of the storm.

The order was repeated by the mate, who sprang to the wheel and assisted in obeying it. Round came the gallant ship with a magnificent sweep, and in another moment she would have been head to wind, when a sudden squall burst upon her broadside and threw her on her beam-ends.

When this happened the mate sprang to the companion-hatch to get an axe, intending to cut the weather-shrouds so that the masts might go overboard and allow the ship to right herself, for, as she then lay, the water was pouring into her. Tom Riggles was, when she heeled over, thrown violently against the mate, and both men rolled to leeward. This accident was the means of saving them for the time, for just then the mizzen rigging gave way, the mast snapped across, and the captain and some of the men who had been hastening aft were swept with the wreck into the sea.

A few minutes elapsed ere Tom and the mate gained a place of partial security on the poop. The scene that met their gaze there was terrible beyond description. Not far ahead the sea roared in irresistible fury on a reef of rocks, towards which the ship was slowly drifting. The light of the moon was just sufficient to show that a few of the men

R. M. Ballantyne

were still clinging to the rail of the forecastle, and that the rigging of the main and foremasts still held fast.

"Have you got the hatchet yet?" asked Tom of the mate, who clung to a belaying-pin close behind him.

"Ay, but what matters it whether we strike the rocks on our beam-ends or an even keel?"

The mate spoke in the tones of a man who desperately dares the fate which he cannot avoid.

"Here! let me have it!" cried Tom.

He seized the hatchet as he spoke and clambered to the gangway. A few strokes sufficed to cut the overstrained ropes, and the mainmast snapped off with a loud report, and the ship slowly righted.

"Hold on!" shouted Tom to a man who appeared to be slipping off the bulwarks into the sea.

As no reply was given, the sailor boldly leapt forward, caught the man by the collar, and dragged him into a position of safety.

"Why, Bill, my boy, is't you?" exclaimed the worthy man in a tone of surprise, as he looked at the face of our hero, who lay on the deck at his feet; but poor Bill made no reply, and it was not until a glass of rum had been poured down his throat by his deliverer that he began to recover.

Several of the crew who had clung to different parts of the wreck now came aft one by one, until most of the survivors were grouped together near the wheel, awaiting in silence the shock which they knew must inevitably take place in the course of a few minutes, for the ship, having righted, now drifted with greater rapidity to her doom.

It was an awful moment for these miserable men! If they could have only vented their feelings in vigorous action it would have been some relief, but this was impossible, for wave after wave washed over the stern and swept the decks, obliging them to hold on for their lives.

At last the shock came. With a terrible crash the good ship struck and recoiled, quivering in every plank. On the back of another wave she was lifted up, and again cast on the cruel rocks. There was a sound of rending wood and snapping cordage, and next moment the foremast was in the sea, tossing violently, and beating against the ship's side, to which it was still attached by part of the rigging. Three of the men who had clung to the shrouds of the foremast were swept overboard and drowned. Once more the wreck recoiled, rose again on a towering billow, and was launched on the rocks with such violence that she was forced forward and upwards several yards, and remained fixed.

Slight although this change was for the better, it sufficed to infuse hope into the hearts of the hitherto despairing sailors. The dread of being instantly dashed to pieces was removed, and with one consent they scrambled to the bow to see if there was any chance of reaching the shore.

Clinging to the fore-part of the ship they found the cook, a negro, whose right arm supported the insensible form of a woman—the only woman on board that ship. She was the wife of the carpenter. Her husband had been among the first of those who were swept overboard and drowned.

"Hold on to her, massa," exclaimed the cook; "my arm

a'most brok."

The mate, to whom he appealed, at once grasped the woman, and was about to attempt to drag her under the lee of the caboose, when the vessel slipped off the rocks into the sea, parted amidships, and was instantly over-whelmed.

For some minutes Bill Bowls struggled powerfully to gain the shore, but the force of the boiling water was such that he was as helpless as if he had been a mere infant; his strength, great though it was, began to fail; several severe blows that he received from portions of the wreck nearly stunned him, and he felt the stupor that preceded death overpowering him, when he was providentially cast upon a ledge of rock. Against the same ledge most of his shipmates were dashed by the waves and killed, but he was thrown upon it softly. Retaining sufficient reason to realise his position, he clambered further up the rocks, and uttered an earnest "Thank God!" as he fell down exhausted beyond the reach of the angry waves.

Soon, however, his energies began to revive, and his first impulse, when thought and strength returned, was to rise and stagger down to the rocks, to assist if possible, any of his shipmates who might have been cast ashore. He found only one, who was lying in a state of insensibility on a little strip of sand. The waves had just cast him there, and another towering billow approached, which would infallibly have washed him away, had not Bill rushed forward and dragged him out of danger.

It proved to be his friend Tom Riggles. Finding that he was not quite dead, Bill set to work with all his energy to revive him, and was so successful that in half-an-hour the sturdy seaman was enabled to sit up and gaze round him with the stupid expression of a tipsy man.

"Come, cheer up," said Bill, clapping him on the back; "you'll be all right in a short while."

"Wot's to do?" said Tom, staring at his rescuer.

"You're all right," repeated Bill. "One good turn deserves another, Tom. You saved my life a few minutes ago, and now I've hauled you out o' the water, old boy."

The sailor's faculties seemed to return quickly on hearing this. He endeavoured to rise, exclaiming—

"Any more saved?"

"I fear not," answered Bill sadly, shaking his head.

"Let's go see," cried Tom, staggering along the beach in search of his shipmates; but none were found; all had perished, and their bodies were swept away far from the spot where the ship had met her doom.

At daybreak it was discovered that the ship had struck on a low rocky islet on which there was little or no vegetation. Here for three weeks the two shipwrecked sailors lived in great privation, exposed to the inclemency of the weather, and subsisting chiefly on shell-fish. They had almost given way to despair, when a passing vessel observed them, took them off, and conveyed them in safety to their native land.

Such was one of the incidents in our hero's career.

R. M. Ballantyne

CHAPTER TWO

COMMENCES THE STORY

About the beginning of the present century, during the height of the war with France, the little fishing village of Fairway was thrown into a state of considerable alarm by the appearance of a ship of war off the coast, and the landing therefrom of a body of blue-jackets. At that time it was the barbarous custom to impress men, willing or not willing, into the Royal Navy. The more effective, and at the same time just, method of enrolling men in a naval reserve force had not occurred to our rulers, and, as a natural consequence, the inhabitants of sea-port towns and fishing villages were on the constant look-out for the press-gang.

At the time when the man-of-war's boat rowed alongside of the little jetty of Fairway, an interesting couple chanced to be seated in a bower at the back of a very small but particularly neat cottage near the shore. The bower was in keeping with its surroundings, being the half of an old boat set up on end. Roses and honeysuckle were trained up the sides of it, and these, mingling their fragrance with the smell of tar, diffused an agreeable odour around. The couple referred to sat very close to each other, and appeared to be engaged in conversation of a confidential nature. One was a fair and rather pretty girl of the fishing community. The other was a stout and uncommonly handsome man of five-and-twenty, apparently belonging to the same class, but there was more of the regular sailor than the fisherman in his costume and appearance. In regard to their conversation, it may be well, perhaps, to let them speak for themselves.

"I tell 'ee wot it is, Nelly Blyth," said the man, in a somewhat stern tone of voice; "it won't suit me to dilly-dally in this here fashion any longer. You've kept me hanging off and on until I have lost my chance of gettin' to be mate of a Noocastle collier; an' here I am now, with nothin' to do, yawin' about like a Dutchman in a heavy swell, an' feelin' ashamed of myself."

"Don't be so hasty, Bill," replied the girl, glancing up at her lover's face with an arch smile; "what would you have?"

"What would I have?" repeated the sailor, in a tone of mingled surprise and exasperation. "Well, I never—no, I never did see nothin' like you women for bamboozlin' men. It seems to me you're like ships without helms. One moment you're beatin' as hard as you can to wind'ard; the next you fall off all of a sudden and scud away right before the breeze; or, whew! round you come into the wind's eye, an' lay to as if you'd bin caught in the heaviest gale that ever blow'd since Admiral Noah cast anchor on Mount Ararat. Didn't you say, not three weeks gone by, that you'd be my wife? and now you ask me, as cool as an iceberg, what I would have! Why, Nelly, I would have our wedding-day fixed, our cottage looked after, our boat and nets bought; in fact, our home and business set a-goin'. And why not at once, Nelly? Surely you have not repented—"

"No, Bill Bowls," said Nelly, blushing, and laying her hand on the arm of her companion, "I have not repented, and never will repent, of having accepted the best man that ever came to Fairway; but—"

The girl paused and looked down.

"There you go," cried the sailor: "the old story. I knew you would come to that 'but,' and that you'd stick there. Why don't you go on? If I thought that you wanted to wait a year or two, I could easily find work in these times; for Admiral Nelson is glad to get men to follow him to the wars, an' Tom Riggles and I have been talkin' about goin' off together."

"Don't speak of *that*, Bill," said the girl earnestly. "I dread the thought of you going to the wars; but—but—the truth is, I cannot make up my mind to quit my mother."

"You don't need to quit her," said Bill; "bring her with you. I'll be glad to have her at my fireside, for your sake, Nell."

"But she won't leave the old house."

"H'm! well, that difficulty may be got over by my comin' to the old house, since the old 'ooman won't come to the noo one. I can rent it from her, and buy up the furniture as it stands; so that there will be no occasion for her to move out of her chair.—Why, what's the objection to that plan?" he added, on observing that Nelly shook her head.

"She would never consent to sell the things,—not even to you, Bill; and she has been so long the head of the house that I don't think she would like to—to—"

"To play second fiddle," put in the sailor. "Very good, but I won't ask to play first fiddle. In fact, she may have first, second, and third, and double bass and trombone, all to herself as far as I am concerned. Come, Nelly, don't let us have any more 'buts'; just name the day, and I'll bear down on the parson this very afternoon."

Leaving them to continue the discussion of this interesting point, we will turn into the cottage and visit the old woman who stood so much in the way of our hero's wishes.

Mrs Blyth was one of those unfortunates who, although not very old, have been, by ill-health, reduced to the appearance of extreme old age. Nevertheless, she had been blessed with that Christian spirit of calm, gentle resignation, which is frequently seen in aged invalids, enabling them to bear up cheerfully under heavy griefs and sufferings. She was very little, very thin, very lame, very old-looking (ninety at least, in appearance), very tremulous, very subdued, and *very* sweet. Even that termagant gossip, Mrs Hard-soul, who dwelt alone in a tumble-down hut near the quay, was heard upon one occasion to speak of her as "dear old Mrs Blyth."

Beside Mrs Blyth, on a stool, engaged in peeling potatoes, sat a young woman who was in all respects her opposite. Bessy Blunt was tall, broad, muscular, plain-looking, masculine, and remarkably unsubdued. She was a sort of maid-of-all-work and companion to the old woman. Mrs Blyth lived in the hope of subduing her attendant—who was also her niece—by means of kindness.

"Who came into the garden just now?" asked Mrs Blyth in a meek voice.

"Who would it be but William Bowls? sure he comes twice every day, sometimes oftener," replied Bessy; "but what's the use? nothing comes of it."

"Something *may* come of it, Bessy," said Mrs Blyth, "if William settles down steadily to work, but I am anxious about him, for he seems to me hasty in temper. Surely, Bessy, you would not like to see our Nell married to an angry man?"

"I don't know about that," replied the girl testily, as she cut a potato in two halves with unnecessary violence; "all I know is that I would like to see her married to Bill Bowls. He's an able, handsome man. Indeed, I would gladly marry him myself if he asked me!"

Mrs Blyth smiled a little at this. Bessy frowned at a potato and said "Humph!" sternly.

Now it happened just at that moment that the press-gang before referred to arrived in front of the cottage. Bessy chanced to look through the window, and saw them pass. Instantly she ran to the back door and screamed "Press-gang," as a warning to Bill to get out of the way and hide himself as quickly as possible, then, hastening back, she seized one of old Mrs Blyth's crutches, ran to the front door, and slammed it to, just as the leader of the gang came forward.

Meanwhile William Bowls, knowing that if he did not make his escape, his hopes of being married speedily would be blasted, turned to leap over the garden wall, but the leader of the press-gang had taken care to guard against such a contingency by sending a detachment round to the rear.

"It's all up with me!" cried Bill, with a look of chagrin, on observing the men.

"Come, hide in the kitchen; quick! I will show you where," cried Nelly, seizing his hand and leading him into the house, the back door of which she locked and barred.

"There, get in," cried the girl, opening a low door in the wall, which revealed the coal-hole of the establishment.

Bill's brow flushed. He drew back with a proud stern look and hesitated.

"Oh, do! for *my* sake," implored Nell.

A thundering rap on the front door resounded through the cottage; the sailor put his pride in his pocket, stooped low and darted in. Nelly shut the door, and leaned a baking-board against it.

"Let us in!" said a deep voice outside.

"Never!" replied Bessy, stamping her foot.

"You had better, dear," replied the voice, in a conciliatory tone; "we won't do you any harm."

"Go along with you—brutes!" said the girl.

"We'll have to force the door if you don't open it, my dear."

"You'd better not!" cried Bessy through the keyhole.

At the same time she applied her eye to that orifice, and instantly started back, for she saw the leader of the gang retire a few paces preparatory to making a rush. There was short time for action, nevertheless Bessy was quick enough to fling down a large stool in front of the door and place herself in an attitude of defence. Next moment the door flew open with a crash, and a sailor sprang in, cutlass in hand. As a matter of course he tripped over the stool, and fell prostrate at Bessy's feet, and the man who followed received such a well-delivered blow from the crutch that he fell on the top of his comrade. While the heroine was in the act of receiving the third she felt both her ankles seized by the man who had fallen first. A piercing yell followed. In attempting to free herself she staggered back and fell, the crutch was wrenched from her grasp, and the whole gang poured over her into the kitchen, where they were met by their comrades, who had just burst in the back door.

"Search close," cried one of these; "there's a big fellow in the house; we saw him run into it."

"You may save yourselves the trouble; there's no man in this house," cried Bessy, who had risen and followed her conquerors, and who now stood, with dishevelled locks, flushed countenance, and gleaming eyes, vowing summary vengeance on the first man she caught off his guard!

As the men believed her, they took care to keep well on their guard while engaged in the search. Poor old Mrs Blyth looked absolutely horror-stricken at this invasion of her cottage, and Nelly stood beside her, pale as marble and trembling with anxiety.

Every hole and corner of the house was searched without success; the floors were examined for trap-doors, and even the ceilings were carefully looked over, but there was no sign of any secret door, and the careless manner in which the bake-board had been leaned against the wall, as well as its small size, prevented suspicion being awakened in that direction. This being the case, the leader of the gang called two of his men aside and engaged in a whispered conversation.

"It's quite certain that he is here," said one, "but where they have stowed him is the puzzle."

"Well, it is indeed a puzzle," replied the leader, "but I've thought of a plan. He may be the father, or brother, or cousin of the household, d'ye see, and it strikes me if we were to pretend to insult the women, that would draw him out!"

"But I don't half like that notion," said one of the men.

"Why not?" asked the other, who wore a huge pair of whiskers, "it's only pretence, you know. Come, I'll try it."

Saying this he went towards old Mrs Blyth and whispered to Nelly—"Don't be frightened, my ducky, we're only a-goin' to try a dodge, d'ye see. Stand by, we won't do you no harm."

The man winked solemnly several times with the view of reassuring Nelly, and then raising his voice to a loud pitch exclaimed—

"Come now, old 'ooman, it's quite plain that there's a feller in this here house, an' as we can't find him nowheres, we've come to the conclusion he must be under your big chair. In coorse we must ask you to git up, an' as ye don't seem to be able to do that very well, we'll have to lift you. So here goes."

The man seized the old woman's chair and shuffled with his feet as though he were about to lift it. Nelly screamed. Bessy uttered a howl of indignation, and rushed upon the foe with teeth and nails ready, but being arrested by a powerful man in the rear, she vented her wrath in a hideous yell.

The success of the scheme was great—much greater, indeed, than had been anticipated. The bake-board fell flat down, the door of the coal-hole burst open, and our hero, springing out, planted a blow on the nose of the big-whiskered man that laid him flat on the floor. Another blow overturned the man who restrained Bessy, and a third was about to be delivered when a general rush was made, and Bill Bowls, being overpowered by numbers, was finally secured.

"Now, my fine fellow," said the leader of the gang, "you may as well go with us quietly, for ye see resistance is useless, an' it only frightens the old woman."

This latter part of the remark had more effect on the unfortunate Bill than the former. He at once resigned himself into the hands of his captors. As he was about to be led away, he turned towards Mrs Blyth, intending to speak, but the poor old woman had fainted, and Nelly's fears for her lover were lost for the moment in her anxiety about her mother. It was not until the party had left the room that the poor girl became fully aware of what was going on.

Uttering a loud cry she rushed towards the outer door. Bill heard the cry, and, exerting himself to the utmost, almost succeeded in overturning the five men who held him.

"Make your mind easy," said one of them; "no harm will

come to the women. We ain't housebreakers or thieves. All fair an' above board we are—true-blue British tars, as would rather swing at the yard-arm than hurt the feelin's of a woman, pretty or ugly, young or old. It's all in the way of dooty, d'ye see? The King's orders, young man so belay heavin' about like that, else we'll heave ye on your beam-ends, lash you hand and futt to a handspike, and carry you aboord like a dead pig."

"Hold on!" cried the man with the big whiskers, who, after having been knocked down, had become emphatic-cally the man with the big nose, "I'll go back an' comfort them a bit: don't you take on so. *I* know all about it—see through it like a double patent hextromogriphal spy-glass. Only goin' on a short cruise, d'ye see? Come back soon with lots o' prize-money; get spliced right off, buy a noo gown with big flowers all over it for the old mother, pension off the stout gal wi' the crutch—all straight; that's the thing ain't it?"

"Don't, don't," entreated Bill earnestly; "don't go for to—to—"

"No fear, young man," replied the sailor, seeing that Bill hesitated; "Ben Bolter ain't the man to do anything that would bring discredit on His Majesty's service, and I bear you no grudge for this," he added, pointing to his swelled nose; "it was given in a good cause, and received in the reg'lar way o' business."

Saying this Ben Bolter ran back to the cottage, where he tried to comfort the women to the best of his power. How he accomplished his mission does not remain on record, but it is certain that he rejoined his party, in little more than five minutes, with sundry new marks of violence on his huge honest face, and he was afterwards heard to remark that some creatures of the tiger species must have been born women by mistake, and that stout young females who had a tendency to use crutches, had better be pensioned off—or, "drownded if possible."

Thus was William Bowls impressed into the Royal Navy. On hearing that his old shipmate had been caught, Tom Riggles at once volunteered into the service, and they were both sent on board a man-of-war, and carried off to fight the battles of their country.

CHAPTER THREE

BILL IS INITIATED INTO
THE DUTIES OF HIS NEW STATION

At the time of which we write, England's battles and troubles were crowding pretty thick upon one another. About this period, Republican France, besides subduing and robbing Switzerland, Italy, Sardinia, and other States, was busily engaged in making preparation for the invasion of England,—Napoleon Bonaparte being in readiness to take command of what was styled the "army of England." Of course great preparations had to be made in this country to meet the invading foe. The British Lion was awakened, and although not easily alarmed or stirred up, he uttered a few deep-toned growls, which showed pretty clearly what the Frenchmen might expect if they should venture to cross the Channel. From John o' Groats to the Land's End the people rose in arms, and in the course of a few weeks 150,000 volunteers were embodied and their training begun.

Not satisfied with threatening invasion, the Directory of France sought by every means to corrupt the Irish. They sent emissaries into the land, and succeeded so well that in May 1798 the rebellion broke out. Troops, supplies, and munitions of war were poured into Ireland by France;

R. M. Ballantyne

but the troops were conquered and the rebellion crushed.

Finding at length that the invasion of England could not be carried out, this pet projection was abandoned, and Napoleon advised the Directory to endeavour to cripple her resources in the East. For the accomplishment of this purpose, he recommended the establishment on the banks of the Nile of a French colony, which, besides opening a channel for French commerce with Africa, Arabia, and Syria, might form a grand military depot, whence an army of 60,000 men could be pushed forward to the Indus, rouse the Mahrattas to a revolt, and excite against the British the whole population of those vast countries.

To an expedition on so grand a scale the Directory objected at first, but the master-spirit who advised them was beginning to feel and exert that power which ultimately carried him to the throne of the Empire. He overcame their objections, and the expedition to Egypt was agreed to.

With characteristic energy and promptitude Napoleon began to carry out his plans, and Great Britain, seeing the storm that was brewing, commenced with equal energy to thwart him. Accordingly, the great Sir Horatio Nelson, at that time rear-admiral, was employed with a squadron to watch the movements and preparations of the French in the Mediterranean.

Such was the state of matters when our hero, Bill Bowls, was conveyed on board the *Waterwitch*, a seventy-four gun frigate, and set to work at once to learn his duty.

Bill was a sensible fellow. He knew that escape from the service, except in a dishonourable manner, was impossible, so he made up his mind to do his duty like a man, and return home at the end of the war (which he hoped would be a short one), and marry Nelly Blyth. Poor fellow, he little imagined what he had to go through before—but hold, we must not anticipate the story.

Well, it so happened that Bill was placed in the same mess with the man whose nose he had treated so unceremoniously on the day of his capture. He was annoyed at this, but the first time he chanced to be alone with him, he changed his mind, and the two became fast friends. It happened thus:—

They were standing on the weather-side of the forecastle in the evening, looking over the side at the setting sun.

"You don't appear to be easy in your mind," observed Ben Bolter, after a prolonged silence.

"*You* wouldn't be if you had left a bride behind you," answered Bill shortly.

"How d'ye know that?" said Ben; "p'r'aps I *have* left one behind me. Anyhow, I've left an old mother."

"That's nothin' uncommon," replied Bill; "a bride may change her mind and become another man's wife, but your mother can't become your aunt or your sister by any mental operation that I knows of."

"I'm not so sure o' that, now," replied Ben, knitting his brows, and gazing earnestly at the forebrace, which happened to be conveniently in front of his eyes; "see here, s'pose, for the sake of argiment, that you've got a mothers an' she marries a second time—which some mothers is apt to do, you know,—and her noo husband has got a pretty niece. Nothin' more nat'ral than that you

R. M. Ballantyne

should fall in love with her and get spliced. Well, wot then? why, your mother is her aunt by vartue of her marriage with her uncle, and so your mother is *your* aunt in consikence of your marriage with the niece—d'ye see?"

Bill laughed, and said he didn't quite see it, but he was willing to take it on credit, as he was not in a humour for discussion just then.

"Very well," said Ben, "but, to return to the p'int—which is, if I may so say, a p'int of distinkshun between topers an' argifiers, for topers are always returnin' to the pint, an' argifiers are for ever departin' from it—to return to it, I say: you've no notion of the pecoolier sirkumstances in which I left my poor old mother. It weighs heavy on my heart, I assure ye, for it's only three months since I was pressed myself, an' the feelin's ain't had time to heal yet. Come, I'll tell 'e how it was. You owe me some compensation for that crack on the nose you gave me, so stand still and listen."

Bill, who was becoming interested in his messmate in spite of himself, smiled and nodded his head as though to say, "Go on."

"Well, you must know my old mother is just turned eighty, an' I'm thirty-six, so, as them that knows the rule o' three would tell ye, she was just forty-four when I began to trouble her life. I was a most awful wicked child, it seems. So they say at least; but I've no remembrance of it myself. Hows'ever, when I growed up and ran away to sea and got back again an' repented—mainly because I didn't like the sea—I tuk to mendin' my ways a bit, an' tried to make up to the old 'ooman for my prewious wickedness. I do believe I succeeded, too, for I got to like her in a way I never did before; and when I used to come home from a cruise—for, of course, I soon went to sea again—I always had somethin' for her from furrin' parts. An' she was greatly pleased at my attentions an' presents—all except once, when I brought her the head of a mummy from Egypt. She couldn't stand that at all—to my great disappointment; an' what made it wuss was, that after a few days they had put it too near the fire, an' the skin it busted an' the stuffin' began to come out, so I took it out to the back-garden an' gave it decent burial behind the pump.

"Hows'ever, as I wos goin' to say, just at the time I was nabbed by the press-gang was my mother's birthday, an' as I happened to be flush o' cash, I thought I'd give her a treat an' a surprise, so off I goes to buy her some things, when, before I got well into the town—a sea-port it was—down comed the press-gang an' nabbed me. I showed fight, of course, just as you did, an floored four of 'em, but they was too many for me an' before I knowed where I was they had me into a boat and aboord this here ship, where I've bin ever since. I'm used to it now, an' rather like it, as no doubt you will come for to like it too; but it *was* hard on my old mother. I begged an' prayed them to let me go back an' bid her good-bye, an' swore I would return, but they only laughed at me, so I was obliged to write her a letter to keep her mind easy. Of all the jobs I ever did have, the writin' of that letter was the wust. Nothin' but dooty would iver indooce me to try it again; for, you see, I didn't get much in the way of edication, an' writin' never came handy to me.

"Hows'ever," continued Ben, "I took so kindly to His Majesty's service that they almost look upon me as an old hand, an' actooally gave me leave to be the leader o' the gang that was sent to Fairway to take you, so that I might have a chance o' sayin' adoo to my old mother."

"What!" exclaimed Bowls, "is your mother the old woman who stops at the end o' Cow Lane, where Mrs Blyth lives, who talks so much about her big-whiskered Ben?"

"That same," replied Ben, with a smile: "she was always proud o' me, specially after my whiskers comed. I thought that p'r'aps ye might have knowed her."

"I knows her by hearsay from Nelly Blyth, but not bein' a native of Fairway, of course I don't know much about the people.—Hallo! Riggles, what's wrong with 'e to-day?" said Bill, as his friend Tom came towards him with a very perplexed expression on his honest face, "not repenting of havin' joined the sarvice already, I hope?"

"No, I ain't troubled about that," answered Riggles, scratching his chin and knitting his brows; "but I've got a brother, d'ye see—"

"Nothin' uncommon in that," said Bolter, as the other paused.

"P'r'aps not," continued Tom Riggles; "but then, you see, my brother's such a preeplexin' sort o' feller, I don't know wot to make of him."

"Let him alone, then," suggested Ben Bolter.

"That won't do neither, for he's got into trouble; but it's a long story, an' I dessay you won't care to hear about it."

"You're out there, Tom," said Bowls; "come, sit down here and let's have it all."

The three men sat down on the combings of the

fore-hatch, and Tom Riggles began by telling them that it was of no use bothering them with an account of his brother Sam's early life.

"Not unless there's somethin' partikler about it," said Bolter.

"Well, there ain't nothin' very partikler about it, 'xcept that Sam was partiklerly noisy as a baby, and wild as a boy, besides bein' uncommon partikler about his wittles, 'specially in the matter o' havin' plenty of 'em. Moreover, he ran away to sea when he was twelve years old, an' was partiklerly quiet after that for a long time, for nobody know'd where he'd gone to, till one fine mornin' my mother she gets a letter from him sayin' he was in China, drivin' a great trade in the opium line. We niver felt quite sure about that, for Sam wornt over partikler about truth. He was a kindly sort o' feller, hows'ever, an' continued to write once or twice a year for a long time. In these letters he said that his life was pretty wariable, as no doubt it was, for he wrote from all parts o' the world. First, he was clerk, he said, to the British counsel in Penang, or some sich name, though where that is I don't know; then he told us he'd joined a man-o'-war, an' took to clearin' the pirates out o' the China seas. He found it a tough job appariently, an' got wounded in the head with a grape-shot, and half choked by a stink-pot, after which we heard no more of him for a long time, when a letter turns up from Californy, sayin' he was there shippin' hides on the coast; and after that he went through Texas an' the States, where he got married, though he hadn't nothin' wotever, as I knows of, to keep a wife upon—"

"But he may have had somethin' for all you didn't know it," suggested Bill Bowls.

R. M. Ballantyne

"Well, p'r'aps he had. Hows'ever, the next we heard was that he'd gone to Canada, an' tuk a small farm there, which was all well enough, but now we've got a letter from him sayin' that he's in trouble, an' don't see his way out of it very clear. He's got the farm, a wife, an' a sarvant to support, an' nothin' to do it with. Moreover, the sarvant is a boy what a gentleman took from a Reformation-house, or somethin' o' that sort, where they put little thieves, as has only bin in quod for the fust time. They say that many of 'em is saved, and turns out well, but this feller don't seem to have bin a crack specimen, for Sam's remarks about him ain't complimentary. Here's the letter, mates," continued Riggles, drawing a soiled epistle from his pocket; "it'll give 'e a better notion than I can wot sort of a fix he's in, Will you read it, Bill Bowls?"

"No, thankee," said Bill; "read it yerself, an' for any sake don't spell the words if ye can help it."

Thus admonished, Tom began to read the following letter from his wild brother, interrupting himself occasionally to explain and comment thereon, and sometimes, despite the adjuration of Bill Bowls, to spell. We give the letter in the writer's own words:—

"My dear mother [it's to mother, d'ye see; he always writes to her, an' she sends the letters to me],—My dear mother, here we are all alive and kicking. My sweet wife is worth her weight in gold, though she does not possess more of that precious metal than the wedding-ring on her finger—more's the pity for we are sadly in want of it just now. The baby, too, is splendid. Fat as a prize pig, capable of roaring like a mad bull, and, it is said, uncommonly like his father. We all send our kind love to you, and father, and Tom. By the way, where *is* Tom? You did not mention him in your last. I fear he is one of these roving fellows whom the Scotch very appropriately style ne'er-do-weels. A bad lot they are. Humph! you're one of 'em, Mister Sam, if ever there was, an' my only hope of ye is that you've got some soft places in your heart."

"Go on, Tom," said Ben Bolter; "don't cut in like that on the thread of any man's story."

"Well," continued Riggles, reading with great difficulty, "Sam goes on for to say—"

"'We thank you for your good wishes, and trust to be able to send you a good account of our proceedings ere long. [You see Sam was always of a cheery, hopeful natur, he was.] We have now been on the place fifteen days, but have not yet begun the house, as we can get no money. Two builders have, however, got the plans, and we are waiting for their sp-s-p-i-f- oh! spiflication; why, wot can that be?'"

"It ain't spiflication, anyhow," said Bolter. "Spell it right through."

"Oh! I've got him, it's *specification*," cried Riggles; "well—"

"'Specification. Many things will cost more than we anticipated. We had to turn the family out who had squatted here, at two days' notice, as we could not afford to live at Kinmonday—that's the nearest town, I s'pose. How they managed to live in the log cabin I do not know, as, when it rained—and it has done so twice since we came, furiously—the whole place was deluged, and we had to put an umbrella up in bed. We have had the roof raised and newly shingled, and are as comfortable as can

R. M. Ballantyne

be expected. Indeed, the hut is admirably adapted for summer weather, as we can shake hands between the logs.

"'The weather is very hot, although there has been much more rain this season than usual. There can be no doubt that this is a splendid country, both as regards soil and climate, and it seems a pity to see such land lying waste and unimproved for so many years. It far surpasses my expectations, both in natural beauty and capabilities. We have a deal of work to do in the way of fencing, for at present everybody's livestock is running over a large part of our land; but we haven't got money to buy fencing! Then we ought to have two horses, for the boy that was sent to me from the Reformatory can plough; but again, we haven't a rap wherewith to buy them. One reason of this is that in a new place a fellow is not trusted at first, and the last two hundred dollars we had went in tools, household furniture, utensils, etcetera. We have been living on credit for an occasional chicken or duck from our neighbours, which makes but a poor meal for three— not to mention baby, being very small—and George, that's the boy, having a tremendous appetite!

"'I walked into town twice to try to get some meat, but although there are ostensibly two butchers, I failed to get any. They actually wanted payment for it! Heigho! how I wish that money grew on the trees—or bread. By the way, that reminds me that there are bread-fruit trees in the South Sea Islands. I think I'll sell the farm and go there. One day I had the good luck to rescue a fine young chicken from the talons of a big hawk, upon which we all made a good meal. I really don't know what we should have done had it not been for the great abundance of blackberries here. They are fine and large, and so plentiful that I can gather a bucketful in an hour. We have made them into jam and pies, and are now drying them for winter use. We have also hazel-nuts and plums by the cart-load, and crab-apples in numbers almost beyond the power of figures to express. There is also a fruit about the size of a lime, which they call here the "May apple," but which I have named "omnifruct," as it combines the flavour of apples, pears, peaches, pine-apples, goose-berries, strawberries, rasps—in fact, it is hard to tell what it does *not* resemble. But after all, this is rather light food, and although very Eden-like living—*minus* the felicity— it does not quite satisfy people who have been used most part of their lives to beefsteak and stout.

"'George came to me a week ago. The little rascal would have been here sooner, but first of all the stage-coach upset, and then he fell asleep and was carried ten miles beyond our clearing, and had to walk back as best he could with a big bundle on his shoulder. He is an uncommonly silent individual. We can hardly get him to utter a word. He does what he is told, but I have first to show him how, and generally end by doing it myself. He appears to be a remarkably dead boy, but my excellent wife has taken him in hand, and will certainly strike some fire out of him if she can't put it into him! She has just gone into town on a foraging expedition, and I fondly hope she may succeed in making a raise of some edibles.

"'I have distinguished myself lately by manufacturing a sideboard and dresser, as well as a table and bench for the female authority, and expect to accomplish a henhouse and a gate next week. You see we work in hope. I fervently wish we could live on the same. However, I'm pretty jolly, despite a severe attack of rheumatism, which has not been improved by my getting up in the night and rushing out in my shirt to chase away trespassing cows and pigs, as we have not got a watch-dog yet.

"When my wife shuts her eyes at night her dreams are of one invariable subject—blackberries! She cannot get rid of the impression, and I have serious fears that we shall all break out in brambles. There are not so many mosquitoes here as I had expected; just enough to keep us lively. How I shall rejoice when we have got a cow! It will be a great saving in butter and milk to our neighbours, who at present supply us with such things on credit! We can raise here wheat, oats, Indian corn, etcetera. The only difficulties are the want of seed and money! But it is unkind in me writing to you, mother, in this strain, seeing that you can't help me in my difficulties. However, don't take on about me. My motto is, "Never give in." Give our love to father, also to Tom. He's a good-hearted fellow is Tom, though I fear he'll never come to much good.—Believe me, your affectionate son, SAM. RIGGLES."

"There," said Tom, folding up the letter; "what d'ye think o' that, mates?"

Tom did not at that time get an answer to his question, for just as he spoke the order was given to beat to quarters for exercise, and in a few minutes the decks were cleared, and every man at his post.

But the order which had been given to engage in mimic warfare, for the sake of training the new hands, was suddenly changed into the command to clear for action in earnest, when the look-out reported a French vessel on the weather-bow. Sail was immediately crowded on the *Waterwitch*, and all was enthusiasm and expectation as they gave chase to the enemy.

CHAPTER FOUR

OUR HERO AND HIS FRIENDS SEE SERVICE

The *Waterwitch* was commanded at this time by Captain Ward, a man possessed of great energy and judgment, united to heroic courage. He had received orders to join that portion of the British fleet which, under Nelson, was engaged in searching for the French in the Mediterranean, and had passed Cape St. Vincent on his way thither, when he fell in with the French vessel.

During the morning a thick fog had obscured the horizon, concealing the enemy from view. When the rising sun dispersed it he was suddenly revealed. Hence the abrupt order on board the *Waterwitch* to prepare for action. As the fog lifted still more, another French vessel was revealed, and it was soon found that the English frigate had two Frenchmen of forty-four guns each to cope with.

"Just as it should be!" remarked Captain Ward, when this was ascertained. "There would have been no glory in conquering one Frenchman equal to my own ship in size!"

The *Waterwitch* was immediately steered towards the ship that was nearest, in the expectation that she would show fight at once, but the French commander, probably wishing to delay the engagement until his other vessel could join him, made sail, and bore down on her. Captain Ward, on perceiving the intention, put on a press of canvas, and endeavoured to frustrate the enemy's design. In this he was only partially successful.

"Surely," said Bill Bowls to his friend Ben Bolter, with whom he was stationed at one of the starboard guns on the main deck, "surely we are near enough now to give 'em a shot."

"No, we ain't," said Tom Riggles, who was also stationed at the same gun; "an' depend on it Cap'n Ward is not the man to throw away his shot for nothin'."

Ben Bolter and some of the other men at the gun agreed with this opinion, so our hero, whose fighting propensities were beginning to rouse up, had to content himself with gazing through the port-hole at the flying enemy, and restrained his impatience as he best could.

At last the order was given to fire, and for an hour after that a running fight was maintained, but without much effect. When, however, the two ships of the enemy succeeded in drawing sufficiently near to each other, they hove to, and awaited the advance of the *Waterwitch*, plying her vigorously with shot as she came on.

Captain Ward only replied with his bow chasers at first. He walked the deck with his hands behind his back without speaking, and, as far as his countenance expressed his feelings, he might have been waiting for a summons to dinner, instead of hastening to engage in an unequal contest.

"Cap'n Ward niver growls much before he bites," said

Patrick Flinn, an Irishman, who belonged to Bowls's mess. "He minds me of a spalpeen of a dog I wance had, as was uncommon fond o' fightin' but niver even showed his teeth till he was within half a yard of his inemy, but, och! he gripped him then an' no mistake. You'll see, messmates, that we won't give 'em a broadside till we're within half pistol-shot."

"Don't take on ye the dooties of a prophet, Paddy," said Ben Bolter, "for the last time ye tried it ye was wrong."

"When was that?" demanded Flinn.

"Why, no longer ago than supper-time last night, when ye said ye had eaten such a lot that ye wouldn't be able to taste another bite for a month to come, an' didn't I see ye pitchin' into the wittles this mornin' as if ye had bin starvin' for a week past?"

"Git along wid ye," retorted Flinn; "yer jokes is as heavy as yerself, an' worth about as much."

"An' how much may that be?" asked Ben, with a grin.

"Faix, it's not aisy to tell. I would need to work it out in a algibrabical calkilation, but if ye divide the half o' what ye know by the double o' what ye don't know, an' add the quarter o' what ye might have know'd—redoocin' the whole to nothin', by means of a compound o' the rule o' three and sharp practice, p'r'aps you'll—"

Flinn's calculation was cut short at that moment by the entrance of a round shot, which pierced the ship's side just above his head, and sent splinters flying in all directions, one of which killed a man at the next gun, and another struck Bill Bowls on the left arm, wounding him slightly.

R. M. Ballantyne

The exclamations and comments of the men at the gun were stopped abruptly by the orders to let the ship fall off and fire a broadside.

The *Waterwitch* trembled under the discharge, and then a loud cheer arose, for the immediate result was that the vessel of the enemy which had hit them was partially disabled—her foretopmast and flying jibboom having been shot away.

The *Waterwitch* instantly resumed her course and while Bill Bowls was busily employed in assisting to reload his gun, he could see that the two Frenchmen were close on their lee bow.

Passing to windward of the two frigates, which were named respectively *La Gloire* and the *St. Denis*, Captain Ward received a broadside from the latter, without replying to it, until he had crossed her bow within musket range, when he delivered a broadside which raked her from stem to stern. He then wore ship, and, passing between the two, fired his starboard broadside into the *Gloire*, and, almost immediately after, his port broadside into the *St. Denis*.

The effect on the two ships was tremendous.

Their sails and rigging were terribly cut up, and several of the yards came rattling down on their decks. The *Gloire*, in particular, had her rudder damaged. Seeing this, and knowing that in her crippled state she could do him no further damage, Captain Ward passed on, sailed round the stern of the *St. Denis*, and, when within six yards of her, sent a broadside right in at her cabin windows. Then he ranged alongside and kept up a tremendous fire.

The Frenchmen stuck to their guns admirably, but the British fired quicker. At such close quarters every shot told on both sides. The din and crash of such heavy artillery was terrific; and it soon became almost impossible to see what was going on for smoke.

Up to this point, although many of the men in the *Waterwitch* had been killed or wounded, only one of those who manned the gun at which Bill Bowls served had been hit.

"It's too hot to last long," observed Flinn, as he thrust home a ball and drew out the ramrod; "run her out, boys."

The men obeyed, and were in the act of pulling at the tackle, when a shot from the enemy struck the gun on the muzzle, tore it from its fastenings, and hurled it to the other side of the deck.

Strange to say, only one of the men who worked it was hurt by the gun; but in its passage across the deck it knocked down and killed three men, and jammed one of the guns on the other side in such a way that it became for a time unserviceable. Ben Bolter and his comrades were making desperate efforts to clear the wreck, when they heard a shout on deck for the boarders. The bowsprit of the *Waterwitch* had by that time been shot away; her rigging was dreadfully cut up, and her wheel smashed; and Captain Ward felt that, if the *St. Denis* were to get away, he could not pursue her. He therefore resolved to board.

"Come along, lads," cried Tom Riggles, on hearing the order; "let's jine 'em."

He seized his cutlass as he spoke, and dashed towards the

R. M. Ballantyne

ladder, followed by Bowls, Bolter, Flinn, and others; but it was so crowded with men carrying the wounded down to the cockpit that they had to pause at the foot.

At that moment a handsome young midshipman was carried past, apparently badly wounded.

"Och!" exclaimed Flinn, in a tone of deep anxiety, "it's not Mister Cleveland, is it? Ah! don't say he's kilt!"

"Not quite," answered the midshipman, rousing himself, and looking round with flashing eyes as he endeavoured to wave his hand in the air. "I'll live to fight the French yet."

The poor boy almost fainted from loss of blood as he spoke; and the Irishman, uttering a wild shout, ran towards the stern, intending to gain the deck by the companion-hatch, and wreak his vengeance on the French. Bill Bowls and Ben Bolter followed him. As they passed the cabin door Bowls said hastily to Bolter, "I say, Ben, here, follow me; I'll show ye a dodge."

He ran into the cabin as he spoke and leaped out upon the quarter gallery, which by that time was so close to the quarter of the *St. Denis* that it was possible to jump from one to the other.

Without a moment's hesitation he sprang across, dashed in one of the windows, and went head foremost into the enemy's cabin, followed by Bolter. Finding no one to oppose them there, they rushed upon deck and into the midst of a body of marines who were near the after-hatchway.

"Down with the frog-eaters!" cried Ben Bolter,

discharging his pistol in the face of a marine with one hand, and cleaving down another with his cutlass.

The "frog-eaters," however, were by no means despicable men; for one of them clubbed his musket and therewith hit Ben such a blow on the head that he fell flat on the deck. Seeing this, Bill Bowls bestrode his prostrate comrade, and defended him for a few seconds with the utmost fury.

Captain Ward, who had leaped into the mizzen chains of the enemy, leading the boarders, beheld with amazement two of his own men on the quarter-deck of the *St. Denis* attacking the enemy in rear. Almost at the same moment he observed the fall of one of them. His men also saw this, and giving an enthusiastic cheer they sprang upon the foe and beat them back. Bill Bowls was borne down in the rush by his friends, but he quickly regained his legs. Ben Bolter also recovered and jumped up. In five minutes more they were masters of the ship—hauled down the colours, and hoisted the Union Jack at the Frenchman's peak.

During the whole course of this action the *Gloire*, which had drifted within range, kept up a galling fire of musketry from her tops on the deck of the *Waterwitch*. Just as the *St. Denis* was captured, a ball struck Captain Ward on the forehead, and he fell dead without a groan.

The first lieutenant, who was standing by his side at the moment, after hastily calling several men to convey their commander below, ordered the starboard guns of the prize to be fired into the *Gloire*. This was done with such effect that it was not found necessary to repeat the dose. The Frenchman immediately hauled down his colours, and the fight was at an end.

R. M. Ballantyne

It need scarcely be said that the satisfaction with which this victory was hailed was greatly modified by the loss of brave Captain Ward, who was a favourite with his men, and one who would in all probability have risen to the highest position in the service, had he lived. He fell while his sun was in the zenith, and was buried in the ocean, that wide and insatiable grave, which has received too many of our brave seamen in the prime of life.

The first lieutenant, on whom the command temporarily devolved, immediately set about repairing damages, and, putting a prize crew into each of the French ships, sailed with them to the nearest friendly port.

The night after the action Bill Bowls, Ben Bolter, and Tom Riggles sat down on the heel of the bowsprit to have a chat.

"Not badly hit?" asked Ben of Bill, who was examining the bandage on his left arm.

"Nothin' to speak of," said Bill; "only a scratch. I'm lucky to have got off with so little; but I say, Ben, how does your head feel? That Mounseer had a handy way o' usin' the handspike. I do believe he would have cracked any man's skull but your own, which must be as thick as the head of an elephant. I see'd it comin', but couldn't help ye. Hows'ever, I saved ye from a second dose."

"It wos pritty hardish," said Ben, with a smile, an' made the stars sparkle in my brain for all the world like the rory borailis, as I've see'd so often in the northern skies; but it's all in the way o' trade, so I don't grumble; the only thing as bothers me is that I can't git my hat rightly on by reason of the bump.

"You've no cause to complain—neither of ye," said Tom Riggles, whose left hand was tied up and in a sling, "for you've lost nothin' but a little blood an' a bit o' skin, whereas I've lost the small finger o' my right hand."

"Not much to boast of, that," said Ben Bolter contemptuously; "why, just think of poor Ned Summers havin' lost an arm and Edwards a leg—not to mention the poor fellows that have lost their lives."

"A finger is bad enough," growled Tom.

"Well, so it is," said Bowls. "By the way, I would advise you to try a little of that wonderful salve invented by a Yankee for such cases."

"Wot salve wos that?" asked Tom gruffly, for the pain of his wound was evidently pretty severe.

"Why, the growin' salve, to be sure," replied Bill. "Everybody must have heard of it."

"*I* never did," said Tom. "Did you, Ben?"

"No, never; wot is it?"

"It's a salve for growin' on lost limbs," said Bill. "The Yankee tried it on a dog that had got its tail cut off. He rubbed a little of the salve on the end of the dog, and a noo tail grow'd on next mornin'!"

"Gammon!" ejaculated Tom Riggles.

"True, I assure ye, as was proved by the fact that he afterwards rubbed a little of the salve on the end of the tail, and a noo dog growed on it in less than a week!"

"H'm! I wonder," said Tom, "if he was to rub some of it inside o' your skull, whether he could grow you a noo set o' brains."

"I say, Bill," interposed Ben Bolter, "did you hear the first lieutenant say where he intended to steer to?"

"I heard somethin' about Gibraltar, but don't know that he said we was goin' there. It's clear, hows'ever, that we must go somewhere to refit before we can be of any use."

"Ay; how poor Captain Ward would have chafed under this delay!" said Bill Bowls sadly. "He would have been like a caged tiger. That's the worst of war; it cuts off good and bad men alike. There's not a captain in the fleet like the one we have lost, Nelson alone excepted."

"Well, I don't know as to that," said Ben Bolter; "but there's no doubt that Admiral Nelson is the man to lick the French, and I only hope that he may find their fleet, and that I may be there to lend a hand."

"Ditto," said Bill Bowls.

"Do," added Tom Riggles.

Having thus expressed their sentiments, the three friends separated. Not long afterwards the *Waterwitch* sailed with her prizes into Gibraltar.

Here was found a portion of the fleet which had been forwarded by Earl St. Vincent to reinforce Nelson. It was about to set sail, and as there was every probability that the *Waterwitch* would require a considerable time to refit, some of her men were drafted into other ships. Among others, our friends Bill Bowls, Ben Bolter, and Tom

Riggles, were sent on board the *Majestic*, a seventy-four gun ship of the line, commanded by Captain Westcott, one of England's most noted captains.

This vessel, with ten line-of-battle ships, set sail to join Nelson, and assist him in the difficult duty of watching the French fleet.

R. M. Ballantyne

CHAPTER FIVE

NELSON HUNTS THE FRENCH

At this time Sir Horatio Nelson had been despatched to the Mediterranean with a small squadron to ascertain the object of the great expedition which was fitting out, under Napoleon Bonaparte, at Toulon.

Nelson had for a long time past been displaying, in a series of complicated and difficult operations in the Mediterranean, those splendid qualities which had already won for him unusual honours and fame, and which were about to raise him to that proud pinnacle which he ultimately attained as England's greatest naval hero. His address and success in matters of diplomacy had filled his superiors and the Government with sentiments of respect; his moral courage in risking reputation and position, with unflinching resolution, by *disobeying* orders when by so doing the good and credit of his country could be advanced, made him an object of dread to some, of admiration to others, while his lion-like animal courage and amiability endeared him to his officers and men. Sailors had begun to feel that where Nelson led the way victory was certain, and those who were ordered to join his fleet esteemed themselves most fortunate.

The defeat of the French armament was considered by the English Government a matter of so great importance, that Earl St. Vincent, then engaged in blockading the Spanish fleet, was directed, if he thought it necessary, to draw off his entire fleet for the purpose, and relinquish the blockade. He was, however, told that, if he thought a detachment sufficient, he was to place it under the command of Sir Horatio Nelson. The Earl did consider a detachment sufficient, and had already made up his mind to give the command to Nelson, being thoroughly alive to his great talents and other good qualities. He accordingly sent him to the Mediterranean with three ships of the line, four frigates, and a sloop of war.

This force was now, by the addition to which we have referred, augmented so largely that Nelson found himself in possession of a fleet with which he might not only "watch" the enemy, but, if occasion should offer, attack him.

He was refitting after a storm in the Sardinian harbour of St. Pietro, when the reinforcements hove in sight. As soon as the ships were seen from the masthead of the Admiral's vessel, Nelson immediately signalled that they should put to sea. Accordingly the united fleet set sail, and began a vigorous search for the French armament, which had left Toulon a short time before.

The search was for some time unsuccessful. No tidings could be obtained of the destination of the enemy for some time, but at length it was learned that he had surprised Malta.

Although his fleet was inferior in size to that of the French, Nelson—and indeed all his officers and men— longed to meet with and engage them. The Admiral,

R. M. Ballantyne

therefore, formed a plan to attack them while at anchor at Gozo, but he received information that the French had left that island the day after their arrival. Holding very strongly the opinion that they were bound for Egypt, he set sail at once in pursuit, and arrived off Alexandria on the 28th of June 1798.

There, to his intense disappointment, he found that nothing had been seen or heard of the enemy. Nelson's great desire was to meet with Napoleon Bonaparte and fight him on the sea. But this wish was not to be gratified. He found, however, that the governor of Alexandria was endeavouring to put the city in a state of defence, for he had received information from Leghorn that the French expedition intended to proceed against Egypt after having taken Malta.

Leaving Alexandria, Nelson proceeded in various directions in search of the French, carrying a press of sail night and day in his anxiety to fall in with them, but being baffled in his search, he was compelled to return to Sicily to obtain fresh supplies in order to continue the pursuit.

Of course Nelson was blamed in England for his want of success in this expedition, and Earl St. Vincent was severely censured for having sent so young an officer on a service so important. Anticipating the objection, that he ought not to have made so long a voyage without more certain information, Nelson said, in vindication of his conduct:—

"Who was I to get such information from? The Governments of Naples and Sicily either knew not, or chose to keep me in ignorance. Was I to wait patiently until I heard certain accounts? If Egypt were their object, before I could hear of them, they would have been in

India. To do nothing was disgraceful; therefore I made use of my understanding. I am before your lordships' judgment; and if, under all circumstances, it is decided that I am wrong, I ought, for the sake of our country, to be superseded; for at this moment, when I know the French are not in Alexandria, I hold the same opinion as off Cape Passaro—that, under all circumstances, I was right in steering for Alexandria; and by that opinion I must stand or fall."

It was ere long proved that Nelson *was* right, and that Earl St. Vincent had made no mistake in sending him on a service so important; for we now know that in all the British fleet there was not another man so admirably adapted for the duty which was assigned to him, of finding, fighting, and conquering, the French, in reference to whom he wrote to the first lord of the Admiralty, "Be they bound to the antipodes, your lordship may rely that I will not lose a moment in bringing them to action!"

Re-victualled and watered, the British fleet set sail on the 25th of July from Syracuse. On the 28th, intelligence was received that the enemy had been seen about four weeks before, steering to the South East from Candia.

With characteristic disregard of the possible consequences to his own fame and interest, in his determination to "do the right," Nelson at once resolved to return to Alexandria. Accordingly, with all sail set, the fleet stood once more towards the coast of Egypt.

Perseverance was at length rewarded. On the 1st of August 1798, about ten in the morning, they sighted Alexandria, and saw with inexpressible delight that the port was crowded with the ships of France.

R. M. Ballantyne

And here we venture to say that we sympathise with the joy of the British on this occasion, and shall explain why we do so.

Not every battle that is fought—however brilliant in military or naval tactics it may be, or in exhibitions of personal prowess—deserves our sympathy. Only that war which is waged against oppression is entitled to respect, and this, we hold, applies to the war in which the British were engaged at that time.

France, under the Directory, had commenced a career of unwarrantable conquest, for the simple purpose of self-aggrandisement, and her great general, Bonaparte, had begun that course of successful warfare in which he displayed those brilliant talents which won for him an empire, constituted him, in the ordinary acceptation of the word, a hero, and advanced France to a high position of tyrannical power. But brilliant talents and success could not free him from the charge of being a wholesale murderer.

To oppose such pretentions and practices was a bounden duty on the part of those who loved justice, just as much as it is the duty of every one who has the power to thwart the designs of, and forcibly overcome, a highwayman or a pirate.

Observe, reader, that we do not intend here to imply an invidious comparison. We have no sympathy with those who hold that England was and always is in favour of fair play, while France was bent on tyranny. On the contrary, we believe that England has in some instances been guilty of the sin which we now condemn, and that, on the other hand, many Frenchmen of the present day would disapprove of the policy of France in the time of

Napoleon the First. Neither do we sympathise with the famous saying of Nelson that "one Englishman is equal to three Frenchmen!" The tendency to praise one's-self has always been regarded among Christian nations as a despicable, or at least a pitiable, quality, and we confess that we cannot see much difference between a boastful man and a boastful nation. Frenchmen have always displayed chivalrous courage, not a whit inferior to the British, and history proves that in war they have been eminently successful. The question whether they could beat us or we could beat them, if tested in a fair stand-up fight with equal numbers, besides being an unprofitable one, is not now before us. All that we are concerned about at present is, that in the war now under consideration the British *did* beat the French, and we rejoice to record the fact solely on the ground that we fought in a righteous cause.

With these remarks we proceed to give an account of one of the greatest naval victories ever achieved by British arms.

CHAPTER SIX

THE BATTLE OF THE NILE

After Napoleon Bonaparte had effected his landing in Egypt, the French fleet was permitted to remain at Alexandria for some time, and thus afforded Nelson the opportunity he had sought for so long.

For many previous days he had been almost unable, from anxiety, to take sleep or food, but now he ordered dinner to be served, while preparations were being made for battle, and when his officers rose to leave the table, he said to them:—

"Before this time to-morrow, I shall have gained a peerage or Westminster Abbey."

The French had found it impossible to enter the neglected and ruined port of Alexandria. Admiral Brueys had, by command of Napoleon, offered a reward of 10,000 livres to any native pilot who would safely convey the squadron in, but not one was found who would venture to take charge of a single vessel that drew more than twenty feet. The gallant admiral was compelled, therefore, to anchor in Aboukir Bay, and chose the strongest position that was possible in the circumstances. He ranged his ships in a compact line of battle, in such a manner that the leading vessel lay close to a shoal, while the remainder of the fleet formed a curve along the line of deep water so that it was thought to be impossible to turn it by any means in a South Westerly direction, and some of the French, who were best able to judge, said that they held a position so strong that they could bid defiance to a force more than double their own. The presumption was not unreasonable, for the French had the advantage of the English in ships, guns, and men, but they had omitted to take into their calculations the fact that the English fleet was commanded by one whose promptitude in action, readiness and eccentricity of resource, and utter disregard of consequences when what he deemed the path to victory lay before him, might have been equalled; but certainly could not have been surpassed, by Bonaparte himself.

The French force consisted of thirteen ships of the line and four frigates, carrying in all 1196 guns and 11,230 men. The English had thirteen ships of the line and a fifty-gun ship, carrying in all 1012 guns and 8068 men. All the English line-of-battle ships were seventy-fours. Three of the French ships carried eighty-eight guns, and one, *L'Orient*, was a monster three-decker with 120 guns.

In order to give the reader a better idea of the forces engaged on both sides, we give the following list of ships. It is right, however, to add that one of those belonging to the English (the *Culloden*) ran aground on a shoal when about to go into action, and took no part in the fight.

R. M. Ballantyne

ENGLISH SHIPS.

	Names	Commanders	Guns	Men
1.	Vanguard	Admiral Nelson, Captain Berry	74	595
2.	Minotaur	Thos. Louis	74	640
3.	Theseus	R.W. Millar	74	590
4.	Alexander	A.J. Ball	74	590
5.	Swiftsure	B Hallowell	74	590
6.	Audacious	D Gould	74	590
7.	Defence	J Peyton	74	590
8.	Zealous	S Hood	74	590
9.	Orion	Sir James Saumarez	74	590
10.	Goliath	Thomas Foley	74	590
11.	Majestic	G.B. Westcott	74	590
12.	Bellerophon	H.D.E. Darby	74	590
13.	Culloden	T Trowbridge	74	590 Not engaged
14.	Leander	T.B. Thomson	50	343
15.	La Mutine, Brig			

FRENCH SHIPS.

	Names	Commanders	Guns	Men	
1.	L'Orient	Admiral Brueys	120	1010	Burnt
2.	Le Franklin		80	800	Taken
3.	Le Tonnant		80	800	Taken
4.	Le Guillaume Tell		80	800	Escaped
5.	Le Conquerant		74	700	Taken
6.	Le Spartiate		74	700	Taken
7.	L'Aquilon		74	700	Taken
8.	Le Souverain Peuple		74	700	Taken

9.	L'Heureux		74	700	Taken
10.	Le Timoleon		74	700	Burnt
11.	Le Mercure		74	700	Taken
12.	Le Genereux		74	700	Escaped
13.	Le Guerrier		74	600	Taken
14.	La Diane (Frigate)		48	300	Escaped
15.	La Justice (Frigate)		44	300	Escaped
16.	L'Artemise (Frigate)		36	250	Burnt
17.	La Serieux (Frigate)		36	250	Dismasted, sunk

Such were the forces that met to engage in deadly conflict on the 1st of August 1798, with not only national but world-wide interest pending on the issue, for the battle of the Nile was one of the leading battles of the world.

When Nelson perceived the position of the enemy, his fertile and active mind at once evolved a characteristic course of action. Where there was room, he said, for an enemy's ship to swing, there was room for one of his to anchor. He therefore at once formed the plan of doubling on the French ships, stationing one of his ships on the bow and another on the quarter of each of the enemy.

Nelson immediately explained his intended course to his officers. It had been his custom during the whole time he was engaged in searching for the French fleet, to have his captains as frequently as possible on board the *Vanguard*, when he explained to them his opinions as to the best mode of attack in all the various positions in which it was possible or probable that the enemy might be found. Hence they knew their commander's tactics so well, that when the hour for action arrived, no time was lost in the tedious operation of signalling orders. He had such confidence in all his officers, that after thoroughly explaining his intended plan of attack, he merely said to them, "Form as is most convenient for mutual support, and anchor by the stern. First gain the victory, and then make the best use of it you can."

When Captain Berry, perceiving the boldness of the plan, said, "If we succeed, what will the world say?" Nelson replied, "There is no *if* in the case; that we shall succeed is certain: who may live to tell the story is a very different question!"

Nelson possessed in an eminent degree the power of infusing into his men the irresistible confidence that animated his own bosom. There was probably not a man in the British fleet who did not sail into Aboukir Bay on that memorable day with a feeling of certainty that the battle was as good as gained before it was begun. The cool, quiet, self-possessed manner in which the British tars went to work at the beginning must have been very impressive to the enemy; for, as they advanced, they did not even condescend to fire a shot in reply to the storm of shot and shell to which the leading ships were treated by the batteries on an island in the bay, and by the broadsides of the whole French fleet at half gunshot-range, the men being too busily engaged in furling the sails aloft, attending to the braces below, and preparing to cast anchor!

Nelson's fleet did not all enter the bay at once, but each vessel lost no time in taking up position as it arrived; and as, one after another, they bore down on the enemy, anchored close alongside, and opened fire, the thunder of the French fleet was quickly and increasingly augmented by the British, until the full tide of battle was reached, and the shores of Egypt trembled under the incessant rolling roar of dreadful war; while sheets of flame shot forth and rent the thick clouds which enwrapped the contending fleets, and hung incumbent over the bay.

An attempt was made by a French brig to decoy the English ships towards a shoal before they entered Aboukir Bay, but it failed because Nelson either knew the danger or saw through the device.

It seemed as if the *Zealous* (Captain Hood) was to have the honour of commencing the action, but Captain Foley passed her in the *Goliath*, and successfully accomplished that feat which the French had deemed impossible, and had done their best to guard against. Instead of attacking the leading ship—the *Guerrier*—outside, he sailed round her bows, passed between her and the shore, and cast anchor. Before he could bring up, however, he had drifted down to the second ship of the enemy's line—the *Conquerant*—and opened fire. It had been rightly conjectured that the landward guns of the enemy would not be manned, or even ready for action. The *Goliath*, therefore, made short and sharp work of her foe. In ten minutes the masts of the *Conquerant* were shot away! The *Zealous* was laid alongside the *Guerrier*, and in twelve minutes that vessel was totally disabled. Next came the *Orion* (Sir J. Saumarez), which went into action in splendid style. Perceiving that a frigate lying farther inshore was annoying the *Goliath*, she sailed towards her, giving the *Guerrier* a taste of her larboard guns as long as they would bear upon her, then dismasted and sunk the frigate, hauled round towards the French line, and anchoring between the *Franklin* and the *Souverain Peuple*, received and returned the fire of both.

In like manner the *Audacious* (Captain Gould) justified her name by attacking the *Guerrier* and *Conquerant* at

R. M. Ballantyne

once, and, when the latter struck passed on to the *Souverain Peuple*.

The unfortunate *Guerrier* was also worthy of her title, for she bore the brunt of the battle. Every ship that passed her appeared to deem it a duty to give her a broadside before settling down to its particular place in the line, and finding its own special antagonist or antagonists—for several of the English ships engaged two of the enemy at once. The *Theseus* (Captain Miller), after bringing down the main and mizzen-masts of the *Guerrier*, anchored inside the *Spartiate* and engaged her.

Meanwhile, on the other side of this vessel, Nelson's ship, the *Vanguard*, bore down on the foe with six flags flying in different parts of the rigging, to guard against the possibility of his colours being shot away! She opened a tremendous fire on the *Spartiate* at half pistol-range. The muscular British tars wrought with heroic energy at the guns. In a few minutes six of these guns, which stood on the fore-part of the *Vanguard's* deck, were left without a man, and three times afterwards were these six guns cleared of men—so terrific was the fire of the enemy.

Other four of the British vessels sailed ahead of the *Vanguard* and got into action. One of these—the *Bellerophon* (Captain Darby)—engaged the gigantic *L'Orient*, which was so disproportionately large that the weight of ball from her lower deck alone exceeded that from the whole broadside of her assailant. The result was that the *Bellerophon* was overpowered, 200 of her men were killed or wounded, all her masts and cables were shot away, and she drifted out of the line. Her place, however, was taken by the *Swiftsure*, which not only assailed the *L'Orient* on the bow, but at the same time opened a steady fire on the quarter of the *Franklin*.

Before this time, however, the shades of night had fallen on the scene. The battle began at half-past six in the evening—half-an-hour afterwards daylight was gone, and the deadly fight was lighted only by the lurid and fitful flashing of the guns.

Those vessels of the English squadron which happened to be in rear were some leagues astern when the fight began, and it was so dark when they entered that extreme difficulty was experienced in getting in. One of these— the *Culloden* (Captain Trowbridge)—sounded carefully as she went, but got aground, where she remained helpless during the action, despite the efforts of the *Leander* and *La Mutine* brig to get her off. She served, however, as a beacon to the *Alexander* and *Swiftsure*.

The latter ship, on entering the bay, fell in with the drifting and disabled *Bellerophon*, which was at first supposed to be one of the enemy, because she did not show the signal ordered by Nelson to be hoisted by his ships at the mizzen peak. This arose, of course, from the masts having been shot away. Captain Hallowell wisely refrained from firing on her, saying that, if she was an enemy, she was too much disabled to escape. He passed on, therefore, and, as we have said, took the station and the duty from which the other had been driven.

The huge *L'Orient* was now surrounded. Captain Ball, in the *Alexander*, anchored on her larboard quarter, and, besides raking her with his guns, kept up a steady fire of musketry on her decks. Captain Thomson also, in the *Leander*, took up such a position that he could fire into her and the *Franklin* at the same time.

Standing in the midst of death and destruction, the hero of the Nile did not escape scathless. He remained unhurt, however, until he knew that victory was certain. The first and second ships of the enemy's line were disabled, as we have said, at the commencement of the action, and the third, fourth, and fifth were taken between eight and nine; so that Nelson could not have much, if any, doubt as to the issue of the battle.

Suddenly he received a wound on the head from a piece of langridge shot, and fell into the arms of Captain Berry. A large flap of skin was cut from the bone and fell over his sound eye,—the other having been lost in a previous engagement. The flow of blood was very great, and, being thus totally blinded, he thought that he had received a mortal wound. He was immediately carried down to the cockpit.

The cockpit of a man-of-war lies in that part of the ship which is below water, and is never visited by the light of day. Being safe also from the visitation of shot or shell, it has been selected as the place to which the wounded are conveyed during an action to have their wounds dressed and limbs amputated by the surgeons—whose hands at such seasons are, as may easily be supposed, much too full. No pen can describe adequately the horrors of that dimly-lighted place, with its flickering lights, glittering knives, bloody tables and decks, and mangled men, whose groans of agony burst forth in spite of their utmost efforts to repress them. Here, in the midst of dead, dying, and suffering men, the great Admiral sat down to wait his turn.

The surgeon was engaged in dressing the wounds of a sailor when he was brought down. On learning who it was that required his services, he quitted the man who was under his hands. "No," said Nelson, refusing his proffered assistance, "no; I will take my turn with my brave fellows." Accordingly, there he remained, persistently refusing aid, until every man who had been previously wounded had been attended to! When his turn came, it was found that his wound was merely superficial and heartfelt was the joy expressed by the wounded men and the crew of the *Vanguard* when this was made known.

But before this had been ascertained, and while he believed himself to be dying, Nelson called the chaplain, and gave him his last remembrance to Lady Nelson, appointed a successor to Captain Berry, who was to go to England with the news of the victory, and made other arrangements in anticipation of his death. But his hour had not yet come. When the surgeon pronounced his hurt to be superficial, he refused to take the rest which was recommended, and at once sent for his secretary to write despatches.

While he was thus engaged, a cry was heard which rose above the din of battle, proclaiming that the *L'Orient* was on fire. In the confusion that followed, Nelson found his way upon deck unassisted, and, to the astonishment of every one, appeared on the quarter-deck, and gave orders to lower the boats, and send relief to the enemy.

But before describing the scene that followed, we shall turn aside for a little to watch more closely the proceedings of Captain Westcott in the *Majestic*, and the personal deeds of Bill Bowls and his messmates.

CHAPTER SEVEN

BATTLE OF THE NILE—CONTINUED

The *Majestic* was one of the four ships which sailed into action in the wake of the Admiral. Our hero, Bill Bowls, and his friend Ben Bolter, were stationed at one of the guns on the larboard side of the main deck. Flinders stood near them. Everything was prepared for action. The guns were loaded, the men, stripped to the waist, stood ready, and the matches were lighted, but as yet no order had been given to fire. The men on the larboard side of the ship stood gazing anxiously through the portholes at the furious strife in which they were about to engage.

"Ah, then! but it's hot work is goin' on," said Flinders, turning to Ben Bolter just after a crash of artillery somewhat louder than usual.

"It's hotter work ye'll see soon, when the Admiral gits into action," said Ben.

"True for ye," answered Flinders; "he's a broth of a boy for fightin'. It's an Irishman he should have been born. Hooroo, my hearties! look out!"

This latter exclamation was drawn forth by the crashing

of a stray shot, which entered the ship close to the spot where they stood, and passed out on the starboard side, sending splinters of wood flying in all directions, without hurting any one.

"There goes the first!" said Bill Bowls, looking up at the ragged hole that was left.

"Faix, but it's not the last!" cried Flinders, as another stray shot hit the ship, wounding one of the men, and sending a splinter so close past the Irishman that it grazed his cheek. "Hooroo, boys! come on, the more the merrier! Sure it's death or victory we'll be havin' in half-an-hour."

At this moment of intense excitement and expectation, when every man's nerves tingled to be called into vigorous action, Ben Bolter saw fit to give Flinders a lecture.

"Ye shouldn't ought to speak misrespectful of death, boy," said he gravely. "He's a rough customer when he gits hold of 'e, an' is sartin sure to have the upper hand. It's my opinion that he'll pay this ship a pretty stiff visit to-night, so you'd better treat him with respect, an' belay yer jokin' —of which yer countrymen are over fond."

To this Flinders listened with a humorous expression about the corners of his eyes, while he stroked his chin, and awaited a pause in order to make a suitable reply, but an exclamation from Bill Bowls changed the subject abruptly.

"Ho! boys," he cried, "there goes the Admiral."

A tremendous crash followed his words, and the *Vanguard* was seen to pour a broadside into the *Spartiate* —as before related.

R. M. Ballantyne

The men of the *Majestic* gazed eagerly at the Admiral's ship, which was almost enveloped in thick smoke as they passed ahead, but an order from Captain Westcott to be ready for action called the attention of every man on his duty. Whatever might have been, at that moment, the thoughts of the hundreds of men on board the *Majestic*, the whole soul and body of every man appeared to be concentrated on his own gun, as he awaited in stern silence the order to act.

It came at last, but somewhat differently from what had been expected. A sudden and peculiar motion was felt in the ship, and it was found that she had got entangled with the main rigging of one of the French vessels astern of the *L'Orient*. Instantly men were sent aloft to cut clear, but before this could be accomplished a perfect storm of shot and shell was sent into them from the towering sides of the three-decker. Men fell on all sides before they had an opportunity of firing a shot; again and again the crushing shower of metal came; spars and masts fell; the rigging was cut up terribly, and in a short time the *Majestic* would certainly have been sunk had she not fortunately managed to swing clear. A moment afterwards Captain Westcott, finding himself close alongside the *Heureux*—the ninth ship of the enemy's line—gave the word to open fire, and Bill Bowls had at last the satisfaction of being allowed to apply a light to the touch-hole of his gun. Seventy-four men had for some time past felt their fingers itching with an almost irresistible desire to do this, and now upwards of thirty of them were allowed to gratify their wish. Instantly the good ship received a shock that caused her to quiver from the trucks to the keel, as her broadside went crashing into the *Heureux*.

No longer was there impatient inaction on board the *Majestic*, for not only did the *Heureux* reply vigorously, but the *Tonnant*—the eighth of the enemy's line—opened fire on their other side. The *Majestic* therefore fought on both sides. Throughout the whole ship the stalwart, half-naked men heaved at the huge guns. Everywhere, from stem to stern, was exhibited in full swing the active processes of sponging out, passing along powder and ball, ramming home the charges, running out, working the handspikes, stepping aside to avoid the recoil—and the whole operation of working the guns, as only British seamen know how to work them! All this was done in the midst of smoke, flame, crashing shot, and flying splinters, while the decks were slippery with human blood, and strewn with dead men, from amongst whom the wounded were raised as tenderly as the desperate circumstances in which they were placed would admit of, and carried below. Many of those who were thus raised never reached the cockpit, but again fell, along with those who bore them.

One of the men at the gun where Bill Bowls was at work was in the act of handing a round shot to Bill, when a ball entered the port-hole and hit him on the head, scattering his brains over the gun. Bill sprang forward to catch him in his arms, but slipped on the bloody deck and fell. That fall saved his life, for at the same moment a musket ball entered the port and passed close over his head, shattering the arm of a poor boy—one of those brave little fellows called powder-monkeys—who was in the act of carrying a cartridge to Ben Bolter. Ben could not delay the loading of the piece to assist the little fellow, who used his remaining strength to stagger forward and deliver the cartridge before he fell, but he shouted hastily to a passing shipmate—

"Here, Davis, carry this poor little chap to the cockpit."

Davis turned and took the boy in his arms. He had almost reached the main hatchway when a shell entered the ship and burst close to him. One fragment killed the boy, and another almost cut Davis in two. They fell and died together.

For a long time this terrible firing at short range went on, and many men fell on both sides. Among others, Captain Westcott was killed. He was the only captain who fell in that battle, and was one who, had his life been spared, would certainly have risen to the highest rank in the service. He had "risen from the ranks," having been the son of a baker in Devonshire, and gained the honourable station in which he lost his life solely through his conspicuous abilities and courage.

Up to this point none of those who are principally concerned in this tale had received any hurt, beyond a few insignificant scratches, but soon after the death of the little boy, Tom Riggles received a severe wound in the leg from a splinter. He was carried below by Bill and Ben.

"It's all over with me," he said in a desponding tone as they went slowly down the ladders; "I knows it'll be a case o' ampitation."

"Don't you go for to git down-hearted, Tom," said Ben earnestly. "You're too tough to be killed easy."

"Well, I *is* tough, but wot'll toughness do for a feller agin iron shot. I feels just now as if a red-hot skewer wos rumblin' about among the marrow of my back-bone, an' I've got no feelin' in my leg at all. Depend upon it, messmates, it's a bad case."

His comrades did not reply, because they had reached the

gloomy place where the surgeons were engaged at their dreadful work. They laid Tom down on a locker.

"Good-bye, lads," said Tom, as they were about to turn away, "p'r'aps I'll not see ye again, so give us a shake o' yer flippers."

Bill and Ben silently squeezed their comrade's hand, being unable to speak, and then hastened back to their stations.

It was about this time that the *L'Orient* caught fire, and when Bill and his friend reached the deck, sheets of flame were already leaping out at the port-holes of the gigantic ship. The sides of the *L'Orient* had been recently painted, and the paint-buckets and oil-jars which stood on the poop soon caught, and added brilliancy to the great conflagration which speedily followed the first outbreak of fire. It was about nine o'clock when the fire was first observed. Before this the gallant French Admiral had perished. Although three times wounded, Brueys refused to quit his post. At length a shot almost cut him in two, but still he refused to go below, and desired to be left to die on his quarter-deck. He was spared the pain of witnessing the destruction of his vessel.

Soon the flames got the mastery, and blazing upward like a mighty torch, threw a strong and appropriate light over the scene of battle. The greater part of the crew of the *L'Orient* displayed a degree of courage which could not be surpassed, for they stuck to their guns to the very last; continuing to fire from the lower deck while the fire was raging above them, although they knew full well the dire and instantaneous destruction that must ensue when the fire reached the magazine.

R. M. Ballantyne

The position and flags of the two fleets were now clearly seen, for it was almost as light as day, and the fight went on with unabated fury until about ten o'clock, when, with a terrific explosion, the *L'Orient* blew up. So tremendous was the shock that it seemed to paralyse the combatants for a little, for both fleets ceased to fire, and there ensued a profound silence, which continued for some time. The first sound that broke the solemn stillness was the splash of the falling spars of the giant ship as they descended from the immense height to which they had been shot!

Of the hundreds of human beings who manned that ship, scarcely a tithe were saved. About seventy were rescued by English boats. The scattered and burning fragments fell around like rain, and there was much fear lest these should set some of the neighbouring vessels on fire. Two large pieces of burning wreck fell into the *Swiftsure*, and a port fire into the *Alexander*, but these were quickly extinguished.

On board the *Majestic* also, some portions of burning material fell. While these were being extinguished, one of the boats was ordered out to do all that was possible to save the drowning Frenchmen. Among the first to jump into this boat were Bill Bowls and Ben Bolter. Bill took the bow oar, Ben the second, and in a few moments they were pulling cautiously amid the debris of the wreck, helping to haul on board such poor fellows as they could get hold of. The work was difficult, because comparative darkness followed the explosion, and as the fight was soon resumed, the thunder of heavy guns, together with the plunging of ball, exploding of shell, and whizzing of chain-shot overhead, rendered the service one of danger as well as difficulty.

It was observed by the men of the *Majestic's* boat that

several French boats were moving about on the same errand of mercy with themselves, and it was a strange as well as interesting sight to see those who, a few minutes before, had been bent on taking each other's lives, now as earnestly engaged in the work of saving life!

"Back your starboard oars," shouted Ben, just as they passed one of the French boats; "there's a man swimming on the port bow—that's it; steady; lend a hand, Bill; now then, in with him."

A man was hoisted over the gunwale as he spoke, and the boat passed onward. Just then a round shot from one of the more distant ships of the fleet—whether English or French they could not tell—struck the water a few yards from them, sending a column of spray high into the air. Instead of sinking, the shot ricochetted from the water and carried away the bow of the boat in passing, whirling it round and almost overturning it. At the same moment the sea rushed in and swamped it, leaving the crew in the water.

Our hero made an involuntary grasp at the thing that happened to be nearest him. This was the head of his friend Ben Bolter, who had been seated on the thwart in front of him. Ben returned the grasp promptly, and having somehow in the confusion of the plunge, taken it into his head that he was in the grasp of a Frenchman, he endeavoured to throttle Bill. Bill, not being easily throttled, forthwith proceeded to choke Ben, and a struggle ensued which might have ended fatally for both, had not a piece of wreck fortunately touched Ben on the shoulder. He seized hold of it, Bill did the same, and then they set about the fight with more precision.

"Come on, ye puddock-eater!" cried Ben, again seizing

Bill by the throat.

"Hallo, Ben!"

"Why, wot—is't you, Bill? Well, now, if I didn't take 'e for a Mounseer!"

Before more could be said a boat was observed rowing close past them. Ben hailed it.

"Ho!" cried a voice, as the men rested on their oars and listened.

"Lend a hand, shipmates," cried Ben, "on yer port bow."

The oars were dipped at once, the boat ranged up, and the two men were assisted into it.

"It's all well as ends well, as I've heerd the play-actors say," observed Ben Bolter, as he shook the water from his garments. "I say, lads, what ship do you belong to?"

"Ve has de honair to b'long to *Le Guillaume Tell*," replied one of the men.

"Hallo, Bill!" whispered Ben, "it's a French boat, an' we're nabbed. Prisoners o' war, as sure as my name's BB! Wot's to be done?"

"I'll make a bolt, sink or swim," whispered our hero.

"You vill sit still," said the man who had already spoken to them, laying a hand on Bill's shoulder.

Bill jumped up and made a desperate attempt to leap overboard, but two men seized him. Ben sprang to the rescue instantly, but he also was overpowered by numbers, and the hands of both were tied behind their backs. A few minutes later and they were handed up the side of the French ship.

When day broke on the morning of the 2nd of August, the firing still continued, but it was comparatively feeble, for nearly every ship of the French fleet had been taken. Only the *Guillaume Tell* and the *Genereux*—the two rear ships of the enemy—had their colours flying.

These, with two frigates, cut their cables and stood out to sea. The *Zealous* pursued, but as there was no other British ship in a fit state to support her, she was recalled; the four vessels, therefore, escaped at that time, but they were captured not long afterwards. Thus ended the famous battle of the Nile, in regard to which Nelson said that it was a "conquest" rather than a victory.

Of thirteen sail of the line, nine were taken and two burnt; and two of their four frigates were burnt. The British loss in killed and wounded amounted to 896; that of the French was estimated at 2000.

The victory was most complete. The French fleet was annihilated. As might be supposed, the hero of the Nile was, after this, almost worshipped as a demigod. It is worthy of remark here that Nelson, as soon as the conquest was completed, sent orders through the fleet that thanksgiving should be returned, in every ship, to Almighty God, for the victory with which He had blessed His Majesty's arms.

R. M. Ballantyne

CHAPTER EIGHT

OUR HERO AND HIS MESSMATE
GET INTO TROUBLE

On the night after the battle, Bill Bowls and Ben Bolter were sent on board a French transport ship.

As they sat beside each other, in irons, and securely lodged under hatches, these stout men of war lamented their hard fate thus—

"I say, Bill, this is wot I calls a fix!"

"That's so, Ben—a bad fix."

There was silence for a few minutes, then Ben resumed—

"Now, d'ye see, this here war may go on for ever so long —years it may be—an' here we are on our way to a French prison, where we'll have the pleasure, mayhap, of spendin' our youth in twirlin' our thumbs or bangin' our heads agin the bars of our cage."

"There ain't a prison in France as'll hold me," said Bill Bowls resolutely.

"No? how d'ye 'xpect to git out—seein' that the walls and doors ain't made o' butter, nor yet o' turnips?" inquired Ben.

"I'll go up the chimbley," said Bill savagely, for his mind had reverted to Nelly Blyth, and he could not bear to think of prolonged imprisonment.

"But wot if they've got no chimbleys?"

"I'll try the winders."

"But if the winders is tight barred, wot then?"

"Why, then, I'll bust 'em, or I'll bust myself, that's all."

"Humph!" ejaculated Ben.

Again there was a prolonged silence, during which the friends moodily meditated on the dark prospects before them.

"If we could only have bin killed in action," said Bill, "that would have been some comfort."

"Not so sure o' that, messmate," said Ben. "There's no sayin' wot may turn up. P'r'aps the war will end soon, an' that's not onlikely, for we've whipped the Mounseers on sea, an' it won't be difficult for our lobsters to lick 'em on land. P'r'aps there'll be an exchange of prisoners, an' we may have a chance of another brush with them one o' these days. If the wust comes to the wust, we can try to break out o' jail and run a muck for our lives. Never say die is my motto."

Bill Bowls did not assent to these sentiments in words,

but he clenched his fettered hands, set his teeth together, and gave his comrade a look which assured him that whatever might be attempted he would act a vigorous part.

A few days later the transport entered a harbour, and a guard came on board to take charge of the prisoners, of whom there were about twenty. As they were being led to the jail of the town, Bill whispered to his comrade—

"Look out sharp as ye go along, Ben, an' keep as close to me as ye can."

"All right, my lad," muttered Ben, as he followed the soldiers who specially guarded himself.

Ben did not suppose that Bill intended then and there to make a sudden struggle for freedom, because he knew that, with fettered wrists, in a strange port, the very name of which they did not know, and surrounded by armed enemies, such an attempt would be utterly hopeless; he therefore concluded, correctly, that his companion wished him to take the bearings (as he expressed it) of the port, and of the streets through which they should pass. Accordingly he kept his "weather-eye open."

The French soldiers who conducted the seamen to prison, although stout athletic fellows, and, doubtless, capable of fighting like heroes, were short of stature, so that the British tars looked down on them with a patronising expression of countenance, and one or two even ventured on a few facetious remarks. Bill Bowls and Ben Bolter, who both measured above six feet in their stockings, towered above the crowd like two giants.

"It's a purty place intirely," said an Irish sailor, with a

smiling countenance, looking round upon the houses, and nodding to a group of pretty girls who were regarding the prisoners with looks of pity. "What may be the name of it, av I may make bowld to inquire?"

The question was addressed to the soldier on his right, but the man paid no attention. So the Irishman repeated it, but without drawing forth a reply.

"Sure, yer a paltry thing that can't give a civil answer to a civil question."

"He don't understand Irish, Pat, try him with English," said Ben Bolter.

"Ah, then," said Pat, "ye'd better try that yersilf, only yer so high up there he won't be able to hear ye."

Before Ben had an opportunity of trying the experiment, however, they had arrived at the jail. After they had passed in, the heavy door was shut with a clang, and bolted and barred behind them.

It is probable that not one of the poor fellows who heard the sound, escaped a sensation of sinking at the heart, but certain it is that not one condescended to show his feelings in his looks.

They were all put into a large empty room, the window of which looked into a stone passage, which was itself lighted from the roof; the door was shut, locked, bolted, and barred, and they were left to their meditations.

They had not remained long there, however, when the bolts and bars were heard moving again.

"What say 'e to a rush, lads?" whispered one of the men eagerly.

"Agreed," said Bill Bowls, starting forward; "I'll lead you, boys."

"No man can fight with his hands tied," growled one of the others. "You'll only be spoilin' a better chance, may-hap."

At that moment the last bolt was withdrawn, and the door swung open, revealing several files of soldiers with muskets, and bayonets fixed, in the passage. This sight decided the question of a rush!

Four of the soldiers entered with the turnkey. The latter, going up to Bill Bowls and Ben Bolter, said to them in broken English:—

"You follows de soldat."

Much surprised, but in silence, they obeyed the command.

As they were going out, one of their comrades said, "Good-bye, mates: it's plain they've taken ye for admirals on account o' yer size!"

"Niver a taste," said the Irishman before mentioned, "'tis bein' led, they are, to exekooshion—"

The remainder of this consolatory suggestion was cut off by the shutting of the door.

After traversing several passages, the turnkey stopped before a small door studded with iron nails, and, selecting one of his huge keys, opened it, while the soldiers ranged up on either side.

The turnkey, who was a tall, powerful man, stepped back, and, looking at Bill, pointed to the cell with his finger, as much as to say, "Go in."

Bill looked at him and at the soldiers for a moment, clenched his fists, and drew his breath short, but as one of the guard quietly brought his musket to the charge, he heaved a sigh, bent his head, and, passing under the low doorway, entered the cell.

"Are we to stop long here, Mister Turnkey?" asked Ben, as he was about to follow.

The man vouchsafed no reply, but again pointed to the cell.

"I've always heered ye wos a purlite nation," said Ben, as he followed his messmate; "but there's room for improvement."

The door was shut, and the two friends stood for a few minutes in the centre of their cell, gazing in silence around the blank walls.

The appearance of their prison was undoubtedly depress-sing, for there was nothing whatever in it to arrest the eye, except a wooden bench in one corner, and the small grated window which was situated near the top of one of the walls.

"What d'ye think o' this?" asked Ben, after some time, sitting down on the bench.

"I think I won't be able to stand it," said Bill, flinging

himself recklessly down beside his friend, and thrusting his hands deep into his trouser pockets.

"Don't take on so bad, messmate," said Ben, in a reproving tone. "Gittin' sulky with fate ain't no manner o' use. As our messmate Flinders used to say, 'Be aisy, an' if ye can't be aisy, be as aisy as ye can.' There's wot I calls sound wisdom in that."

"Very true, Ben; nevertheless the sound wisdom in *that* won't avail to get us out o' *this*."

"No doubt, but it'll help us to bear this with equablenimity while we're here, an' set our minds free to think about the best way o' makin' our escape."

At this Bill made an effort to throw off the desperate humour which had taken possession of him, and he so far succeeded that he was enabled to converse earnestly with his friend.

"Wot are we to do?" asked Bill gloomily.

"To see, first of all, what lies outside o' that there port-hole," answered Ben. "Git on my shoulders, Bill, an' see if ye can reach it."

Ben stood against the wall, and his friend climbed on his shoulders, but so high was the window, that he could not reach to within a foot of it. They overcame this difficulty, however, by dragging the bench to the wall, and standing upon it.

"I see nothin'," said Bill, "but the sky an' the sea, an' the prison-yard, which appears to me to be fifty or sixty feet below us."

"That's not comfortin'," observed Ben, as he replaced the bench in its corner.

"What's your advice now?" asked Bill.

"That we remain on our good behaviour a bit," replied Ben, "an' see wot they means to do with us, an' whether a chance o' some sort won't turn up."

"Well, that's a good plan—anyhow, it's an easy one to begin with—so we'll try it for a day or two."

In accordance with this resolve, the two sailors called into play all the patience, prudence, and philosophy of which they were possessed, and during the three days that followed their incarceration, presented such a meek, gentle, resigned aspect; that the stoniest heart of the most iron-moulded turnkey ought to have been melted; but the particular turnkey of that prison was made of something more or less than mortal mould, for he declined to answer questions,—declined even to open his lips, or look as if he heard the voices of his prisoners, and took no notice of them farther than to fetch their food at regular intervals and take away the empty plates. He, however, removed their manacles; but whether of his own good-will or by order they did not know.

"Now, Ben," said Bill on the evening of the third day, as they sat beside each other twirling their thumbs, "this here sort o' thing will never do. I mean for to make a dash when the turnkey comes in the mornin'; will you help me?"

"I'm yer man," said Ben; "but how d'ye mean to set about it?"

"Well, somewhat in this fashion:—W'enever he opens the door I'll clap my hand on his mouth to stop his pipe, and you'll slip behind him, throw yer arms about him, and hold on till I tie a handkerchief over his mouth. Arter that we'll tie his hands and feet with whatever we can git hold of—his own necktie, mayhap—take the keys from him, and git out the best way we can."

"H'm; but wot if we don't know the right turnin's to take, an' run straight into the jaws of other turnkeys, p'r'aps, or find other doors an' gates that his bunch o' keys won't open?"

"Why, then, we'll just fail, that's all; an' if they should scrag us for it, no matter."

"It's a bad look-out, but I'll try," said Ben.

Next morning this plan was put in execution. When the turnkey entered the cell, Bill seized him and clapped his hand on his mouth. The man struggled powerfully, but Ben held him in a grasp so tight that he was as helpless as an infant.

"Keep yer mind easy, Mounseer, we won't hurt 'e," said Ben, while his comrade was busy gagging him.

"Now, then, lift him into the corner," whispered Bill.

Ben and he carried the turnkey, whom they had tied hand and foot with handkerchiefs and neckties, into the interior of the cell, left him there, locked the door on him, and immediately ran along the passage, turned a corner, and came in sight of an iron grating, on the other side of which sat a man in a dress similar to that of the turnkey they had left behind them. They at once drew back and tried to conceal themselves, but the man had caught sight of them, and gave the alarm.

Seeing that their case was desperate, Bill rushed at the grating with all his force and threw himself heavily against it. The whole building appeared to quiver with the shock; but the caged tiger has a better chance of smashing his iron bars than poor Bill Bowls had. Twice he flung his whole weight against the barrier, and the second time Ben helped him; but their efforts were in vain. A moment later and a party of soldiers marched up to the grating on the outside. At the same time a noise was heard at the other end of the passage. Turning round, the sailors observed that another gate had been opened, and a party of armed men admitted, who advanced with levelled muskets.

Seeing this, Bill burst into a bitter laugh, and flung down the keys with a force that caused the long passage to echo again, as he exclaimed—

"It's all up with us, Ben. We may as well give in at once."

"That's so," said Ben sadly, as he suffered himself to be handcuffed, after which he and his companion in misfortune were conducted back to their cell.

R. M. Ballantyne

CHAPTER NINE

BILL AND BEN SET THEIR BRAINS TO STEEP WITH UNCONQUERABLE PERSEVERANCE

In its slow but steady revolution, the wheel of fortune had now apparently brought Bill Bowls and Ben Bolter to the lowest possible point; and the former of these worthies consoled himself with the reflection that, as things could scarcely get worse with them, it was probable they would get better. His friend disputed this point.

"It's all very well," said Ben, crossing his legs and clasping his hands over his knees, as he swayed himself to and fro, "to talk about havin' come to the wust; but we've not got to that p'int by a long way. Why, suppose that, instead o' bein' here, sound in wind and limb, though summat unfort'nate in regard to the matter o' liberty,— suppose, I say, that we wos lyin' in hospital with our right legs an' mayhap our left arms took off with a round shot."

"Oh, if you go for to *supposin'*," said Bill, "you may suppose anything. Why not suppose at once that we was lyin' in hospital with both legs and arms took off by round shot, an' both eyes put out with canister, an' our heads an' trunks carried away by grape-shot?"

"I didn't suppose that," said Ben quietly, "because that would be the best instead o' the wust state we could come to, seein' that we'd know an' care nothin' about it. Hows'ever, here we are, low enough, an' havin' made an assault on the turnkey, it's not likely we'll get much favour at the hands of the Mounseers; so it comes to this, that we must set our brains to steep, an' see if we can't hit upon some dodge or other to escape."

"That's what we must do," assented Bill Bowls, knitting his brows, and gazing abstractedly at the blank wall opposite. "To git out o' this here stone jug is what I've set my heart on, so the sooner we set about it the better."

"Just so," said Ben. "Well, then, let's begin. Wot d'ye propose fust?"

To this Bill replied that he must think over it. Accordingly, he did think over it, and his comrade assisted him, for the space of three calendar months, without any satisfactory result. But the curious thing about it was that, while these men revolved in their minds every conceivable plan with unflagging eagerness, and were compelled to give up each, after brooding over it for a considerable time, finding that it was unworkable, they were not dispirited, but rather became more intense in their meditations, and ingenious as well as hopeful in their devisings.

"If we could only git hold of a file to cut a bar o' the winder with, an' a rope to let ourselves down with, I think we could manage to git over the walls somehow."

"If we was to tear our jackets, trousers, vests, and shirts into strips, an' make a rope of 'em, it might be long enough," suggested Bill.

R. M. Ballantyne

"That's so, boy, but as we would be stark naked before we got it finished, I fear the turnkey would suspec' there wos somethin' wrong somehow."

Ben Bolter sighed deeply as he spoke, because at that moment a ray of sunshine shot through the little window, and brought the free fresh air and the broad blue sea vividly to his remembrance. For the first time he experienced a deep sinking of the heart, and he looked at his comrade with an expression of something like despair.

"Cheer up," said Bill, observing and thoroughly understanding the look. "Never say die, as long as there's a—shot—in—"

He was too much depressed and listless to finish the sentence.

"I wonder," resumed Ben, "if the Mounseers treat all their prisoners of war as bad as they treat us."

"Don't think they do," replied Bill. "I've no doubt it's 'cause we sarved 'em as we did when they first put us in quod."

"Oh, if they would only give us summat to do!" exclaimed Ben, with sudden vehemence.

It seemed as if the poor fellow's prayer were directly answered, for at that moment the door opened, and the governor, or some other official of the prison, entered the cell.

"You must vork," he said, going up to Bill.

"We'll be only too glad to work, yer honour, if you'll give

us work to do."

"Ver' good; fat can you vork?"

"We can turn handy to a'most anything, yer honour," said Ben eagerly.

It turned out, however, after a considerable amount of talk, that, beyond steering a ship, reefing topsails, splicing ropes, tying every species of complex knot, and other nautical matters, the two seamen could not claim to be professionally acquainted with any sort of handicraft. Somewhat discomfited, Ben at last said with a perplexed air—

"Well, yer honour, we'll try anything ye choose to put us at. I had a brother once who was a sort of tinker to trade, an' great at mendin' pots, pans, old umbrellas, and the like. I wos used to help him when a boy. P'r'aps if yer honour, now, has got a old umbrella as wants refittin', I might try my hand on that."

The governor smiled. "Vell, I do tink I have von old omberilla. You sall try for to mend him."

Next day saw Bill and Ben surrounded by tools, scraps of wood and whalebone, bits of brass and tin, etcetera, busy as bees, and as happy as any two children who have invented a new game.

Ben mended the umbrella admirably. At the same time, Bill fashioned and carved two or three paper-knives of wood with great neatness. But when it was discovered that they could sew sail-cloth expeditiously and well, a quantity of that material was given to them, and they were ordered to make sacks. They set to work accordingly, and made sack after sack until they grew so wearied of the monotonous work that Ben said it made him wish to sit down in sackcloth and ashes; whereupon Bill remarked that if the Mounseers would only give them the sack altogether, it would be very much to their credit.

Soon the imprisoned mariners began again to plot and plan their escape. Of course they thought of making ropes of the sail-cloth and twine with which they wrought, but as the turnkey took the material away every night, and brought it back every morning, they gave up this idea, as they had given up many other ideas before.

At last, one afternoon, Bill looked up from his work, hit his thigh a slap which produced a pistol-shot crack that echoed up into the high ceiling of the cell, as he exclaimed, "I've got it!"

"I hope you'll give us a bit of it, then," said Ben, "if it's worth havin'."

"I'll give you the benefit of it, anyhow," said Bill, throwing down his tools and eagerly beginning to expound the new plan which had struck him and caused him to strike his thigh. It was to this effect:—

That they should beg the turnkey to let them have another old umbrella to work at by way of recreation, as the sack-making was rather monotonous; that, if they should be successful in prevailing on him to grant their request, they should work at the umbrella very slowly, so as to give them time to carry out their plan, which was to form a sort of parachute by adding sail-cloth round the margin of the umbrella so as to extend it to twice its circumference. After it should be finished they were to seize a fitting opportunity, cut the bars of their window, and, with the machine, leap down into the yard below.

"Wot!" exclaimed Ben, "jump together!"

"Ay, why not, Ben? Sink or swim, together, boy."

"Very true, but I've got my doubts about flyin' together. Better do it one at a time, and send the umbrella up by means of a piece of twine."

"Well, we might do it in that way," said Bill; "but what d'ye think o' the plan?"

"Fuss rate," said Ben, "we'll try it at once."

In accordance with this resolution, Ben made his petition that night, very humbly, to the turnkey, who at first turned a deaf ear to him, but was finally prevailed on to fetch them one of his own umbrellas to be repaired. It happened to be a very large one of the good old stout and bulgy make, and in this respect was the better suited to their purpose. All the tools necessary for the work of repair were supplied except a file. This, however, was brought to them, when Ben pointed out, with much earnestness, that if he had such an implement he could clean up and beautify the ivory handle to such an extent that its owner would not recognise it.

This device of improving the ivory handle turned out to be a happy hit, for it enabled Ben to keep the umbrella much longer by him than would otherwise have been possible, for the purpose of covering it with elaborate and really beautiful carving, the progress of which was watched by the turnkey with much interest from day to day.

Having gained their end the sailors wrought with inde-
fatigable zeal, and resolutely overcame the difficulties
that met them from time to time. Each day they dragged
the bench under the window. Ben got upon it, and Bill
climbed on his shoulders, by which means he could just
reach the iron grating of the window, and there, for half-
an-hour at a time, he cautiously used the file. They
thought this enough of time to bestow on the work,
because the bars could be easily filed through before the
parachute was ready.

In the preparation of the umbrella, the first difficulty that
met them was how they were to conceal their private
work when the turnkey came in the evenings to take away
their materials for sack-making. After some examination
they discovered a plank in the floor, in the corner where
they were wont to sleep, which was loose and easily
forced up with one of Bill's unfinished paper-knives,
which he made very strong for this special purpose!
Beneath there was sufficient room to stow away the cloth
with which they fashioned the additional breadth to the
umbrella. To have cabbaged at one time all the sail-cloth
that was required would have risked discovery; they
therefore appropriated small scraps each day, and sewed
these neatly together until they had enough. Soon they
had a ring of canvas formed, into the centre of which the
umbrella fitted exactly, and this ring was so cut and sewn
in gores that it formed a continuation of the umbrella,
which was thus made to spread out and cover a space of
about nine or ten feet in diameter. All round the extremity
or margin of the ring, cords of twisted twine were fixed,
at intervals of about six inches. There were about sixty of
these cords or stays, all of which met and were fastened at
the end of the handle. A stout line, made of four-ply
twine, was fastened at the top of the umbrella, and passing
through a small hole in it was tied round the whalebones

inside, and twisted down the stick to the handle, to which it was firmly secured. By this means the whole machine was, as it were, bound together.

All these additionals and fixings had, however, to be so constructed that they could be removed, or affixed with some rapidity, for there was always before the sailors the chance that the turnkey might look in to observe how their work was progressing.

Indeed one afternoon they were almost discovered at work on the parachute. The turnkey was heard coming along the passage when Ben was in the act of fitting on the new appendages, and the key was actually in the door before the last shred of them was thrust into the hole in the floor, and the loose plank shut down! Ben immediately flung several of the sacks over the place, and then turning suddenly round on his comrade began to pommel him soundly by way of accounting for the flushed condition of his countenance.

Thus taken by surprise, Bill returned the blows with interest, and the combatants were separated by the turnkey when in a rather breathless condition!

"If you do so more agin, you sall go separate," said the turnkey.

The mere thought of separation at such a moment struck like a chill to the hearts of the sailors, who forthwith shook hands, and vowed earnestly that they would "never do it again." In order to conciliate the man, Ben took up the umbrella, and pointing to the beautifully carved handle said—

"You see it's all but finished, and I'm very anxious to git it

R. M. Ballantyne

done, so if you'll let me keep it by me all to-night, I'll work as long as I can see, and be at it the first thing in the morning."

The man, pleased at the unusual interest which Ben took in the worn-out piece of goods, agreed to let him keep it by him. After carrying away all the other materials, and looking round to see that all was right, he locked them up for the night.

Left to themselves, they at once began to prepare for action. They drew forth all the different parts of the parachute (for such it really was, although the machine so named had never been seen, but only heard of, by the seamen), and disposed them in such a manner beside the hole in the floor as to be ready at a moment's notice, either to be fitted on to the umbrella or thrust back into the place of concealment.

Their manacles had been taken off at the time they began to work, so that these were no longer impediments in the way.

"Now, Bill, are the bars sure to give way, d'ye think?"

"Sartin sure," said Bill; "they're holdin' by nothin' thicker than a pin."

"Very good, then, let's go to work. In an hour or so it will be dark enough to try our flyin' machine, and then good-bye to France—or to the world. It's neck or nothin', d'ye see?"

"All right," answered Bill.

They sat down to work in good earnest. The spreading

rim of canvas, instead of being tagged on as on former occasions, was now sewn securely to the umbrella, and when the latter was expanded, the canvas hung down all round it, and the numerous stays hung quite loose. Ben expected that the rapidity of the descent would suddenly expand this appendage, and check the speed. The ends of the loose cords were gathered up and fastened to the handle, as was also the binding-cord before referred to— all of which was done with that thoroughness of workmanship for which sailors are celebrated.

Then a stout cord was fastened to one of the stanchions of the window, which had been left uncut for the purpose.

When everything was ready the adventurous sailors began to experience all the anxiety which is inseparable from an action involving much danger, liability to frustration, and requiring the utmost caution combined with energy.

They waited until they thought the night was at its darkest. When all sounds around them had ceased, they took off their shoes and carefully lifted the bench to the wall under the window. Ben went up first by mounting on Bill's shoulders. With one powerful wrench he pulled the iron framework of the window into the room, and handed it down to Bill, who stooped a little and placed it gently against the wall. His comrade then thrust his head and shoulders out at the window, and while in that awkward position spread his jacket over the sill. This was intended to protect the cord which was fastened to the top of the umbrella, and by which it was to be drawn up after his descent.

When this was done, Bill clambered up by the cord which hung from the uncut stanchion, and pushed the umbrella past Ben's body until he got hold of the end of it, and

R. M. Ballantyne

drew it out altogether. Bill then descended into the cell, having the small cord in his hand, and watched the motions of his comrade with intense anxiety.

The window was so small that Ben could barely get his head and shoulders through it. There was no possibility of his getting on his feet or his knees to make a leap. The only course that remained for him, therefore, was to expand the umbrella, hold on tight, and then wriggle out until he should lose his balance and fall head foremost! It was an awful position. Bold though the seaman was, and desperate the circumstances, his strong frame quivered when he gazed down and felt himself gradually toppling. The height he knew to be little short of sixty feet, but in the dark night it appeared an abyss of horrible profundity. A cold sweat broke out upon him, and for one moment he felt an almost irresistible tendency to let go the umbrella and clutch the window-sill, but he was too late. Like lightning he shot down for a couple of yards; then the parachute expanded and checked him with such violence, as he swung round, that he nearly lost his hold and was thrown into a horizontal position—first on one side, then on the other. Finally, he reached the ground with a shock that almost took away his breath. He sat still for a moment or two, then rose slowly and shook himself, to ascertain whether he were still alive and sound! Immediately after he examined the parachute, found it all right, and gave his comrade the signal—a couple of tugs at the cord—to haul up.

Bill was scarcely less agitated than his friend. He had seen Ben's legs disappear with a suddenness that told eloquently of his having taken flight, and stood in the cell above listening intently, while large drops of perspiration coursed down his face. On feeling the tug at the string, a mountain appeared to be lifted off his chest. Carefully he pulled up the umbrella. When it showed its point above the window-sill he clambered up and went through the same terrible ordeal. He was not, however, so fortunate as his friend, for, when he jumped, three of the stays gave way, which had the effect of slightly deranging the motion of the umbrella, and he came to the ground with such violence that he lay stunned and motionless, leading his horrified comrade to fear that he was killed. In a few minutes, however, he revived, and, on examination, found that no bones had been broken.

"Now, Ben, what next?" said Bill, getting up, and giving himself a shake.

"The wall," said Ben, "can't be far from where we stand. If there wos only a bit of moonshine it would help us."

"Better as it is," whispered Bill, groping about, for the night was so intensely dark that it was scarcely possible to see a yard. "I knows the way to the harbour, if we only manage to get out.—Ah, here's the wall, but it's an oncommon high one!"

This was indeed too true. The top of the wall was faintly visible like a black line across the dark sky, and when Ben mounted on Bill's shoulders, it was found that he could only reach to within three feet of the bristling iron spikes with which it was surmounted. For half-an-hour they groped about, and made the discovery that they were in a small enclosure with bare walls of fifteen feet in height around them, and not a projection of any kind large enough for a mouse to lay hold of! In these circumstances many men would have given way to despair; but that was a condition of mind which neither of our tars ever thought of falling into. In the course of their explorations they came against each other, and immediately began an

R. M. Ballantyne

animated conversation in whispers, the result of which was that they groped for the umbrella, and, having found it, cut off all the cords about it, with which they proceeded to plait a rope strong enough to bear their weight. They sat down in silence to the work, leaning against the prison wall, and wrought for a full hour with the diligence of men whose freedom depends on their efforts. When finished, the rope was found to be about a yard too short for their purpose; but this defect was remedied by means of the canvas of their parachute, which they tore up into strips, twisted into an additional piece of rope, and spliced it to the other. A large loop was made on the end of it. Going once more to the wall, Ben mounted on Bill's shoulders, and threw the loop over the top of the wall; it caught, as had been expected, on one of the iron spikes. Ben then easily hauled himself up, hand over hand, and, getting hold of two spikes, raised himself so that he could see over the wall. Immediately after he descended.

"I sees nothin', Bill, so we must just go over and take our chance."

Bill agreed. Ben folded his coat, and ascending again, spread it over the spikes, so that he could lean on them with his chest without being pierced. Having re-ascended, Bill followed; the rope was then hauled up, and lowered on the other side. In another moment they slipped down, and stood on the ground.

"Now, the question is, where are we!" whispered Bill. "P'r'aps we're only in another yard after all."

The sound of footsteps pacing slowly towards them was heard at that moment.

"I do believe," whispered Bill, in an excited tone, "that we've got into the street, an' that's the sentry. Let's bolt."

"We can't bolt," said Ben, "'cause, if I took my bearin's right, he's between us an' the shore, an' it would be of no manner o' use boltin' into the country to be hunted down like a couple of foxes."

"Then we'll floor him to begin with," whispered Bill.

"That's so," said Ben.

The sentry approached, and the sailors drew up close against the wall. Presently his dark form became faintly visible. Bill rushed at him at once, and delivered a blow that might have felled an ox at the spot where he supposed his chest was, sending the man back almost heels over head, while his arms rattled on the pavement. Instantly there were heard the sounds of opening locks, bolts, and bars. The two friends fled, and shouts were heard behind them, while lights flashed in various directions.

"This way, Bill," cried Ben, turning down a narrow lane to avoid a lamp which came in sight when they turned a corner. A couple of belated and drunken French fisher-men happened to observe them, and gave chase. "Hold on, Ben, let's drop, and trip 'em up," said Bill.

"All right," replied Ben; "down with 'e."

They stopped suddenly, and squatted as low as possible. The lane was very narrow; the fishermen were close behind; they tumbled right over them, and fell heavily on their faces. While they were rising, our heroes knocked them both insensible, and hastily appropriating their coats

R. M. Ballantyne

and red caps put them on as they ran. By this time a crowd of fishermen, sailors, and others, among whom were a few soldiers and turnkeys with lanterns, were pursuing the fugitives as fast as was possible in so dark a night. Bill suggested that they should turn into a dark corner, and dodge them. The suggestion was acted on at once. They dashed round the first corner they came to, and then, instead of continuing their flight, turned sharp to the left, and hid in a doorway. The pursuers came pouring round the corner, shouting wildly. When the thickest of the crowd was opposite their place of concealment, Bill and Ben rushed into the midst of them with a shout, imitating the tones of the Frenchmen as nearly as possible, but taking care to avoid the use of word, and thus they joined in the pursuit! Gradually they fell behind, as if out-run, and, when they found themselves in rear, turned about, and made off in the opposite direction, then, diverging to the left, they headed again towards the shore, ran down to the beach, and leaped into the first boat they came to.

It happened to be a very small one,—a sort of dinghy. Ben thought it was too small, and was about to leap out and search for a larger, when lights suddenly appeared, and the shouts of the pursuers—who had discovered the *ruse*—were heard as they approached.

"Shove off, Ben!"

"Hurrah, my hearties!" cried the seaman with a stentorian shout as he seized an oar.

Next moment the little boat was flying over the smooth water of the port, the silence of which was now broken by exclamations and cries from the shipping in reply to those from the shore; while the splashing of oars were heard in all directions as men leaped into boats and rowed about at random. Darkness favoured the Englishmen, but it also proved the cause of their being very nearly re-captured; for they were within two yards of the battery at the mouth of the harbour before they observed it, and swerved aside just in time to avoid a collision. But they had been seen, and a random discharge of musketry followed. This was succeeded by the sudden blaze of a blue light, which revealed the whole port swarming with boats and armed men,—a sight which acted so powerfully on the warlike spirits of the sailors that they started up simultaneously, flung their red caps into the air, and gave vent to a hearty British cheer, which Ben Bolter followed up as they resumed the oars, with "Old England for ever! farewell, Mounseers!"

The blue light went out and left everything in darkness thicker than ever, but not before a rapid though ineffective discharge of musketry had been made from the battery. Another blue light, however, showed that the fugitives were getting rapidly out to sea beyond the range of musketry, and that boats were leaving the port in chase. Before the light expired a cloud of smoke burst from the battery, and the roar of a heavy gun rushed over the sea. An instant later and the water was torn up by grape-shot all round the little boat; but not a ball touched them save one, which struck Bill Bowls on the left hand and cut off his thumb.

"I think there's a mast and sail in the bottom of the boat, and here comes a breeze," said Ben; "give me your oar, and try to hoist it, Bill."

Without mentioning his wound, our hero did as he was bid; and not until the boat was leaping over the ruffled sea did he condescend to bind up the wounded hand with his

R. M. Ballantyne

necktie. Soon they were beyond the range of blue lights and artillery.

"Have 'e any notion what course we're steerin'?" inquired Bill.

"None wotsomediver," answered Ben.

Soon after that, however, the sky cleared a little, and Bill got sight of part of the constellation of the Great Bear. Although the pole-star was not visible, he guessed pretty nearly its position, and thus ascertained that the breeze came from the south-west. Trimming the lug-sail accordingly, the tars turned the prow of the little craft to the northward, and steered for the shores of old England.

About a year after this stirring incident, a remarkably noisy party was assembled at tea in the prim little parlour of Mrs Blyth's cottage in Fairway. Besides the meek old soul herself, there were present on that occasion our old friends Ben Bolter and Tom Riggles, the latter of whom flourished a wooden stump instead of a right leg, and wore the garb of a Greenwich pensioner. His change of circumstances did not appear to have decreased his love for tobacco. Ben had obtained leave of absence from his ship for a day or two, and, after having delighted the heart of his old mother by a visit, had called at the cottage to pay his respects to his old messmate, little thinking that he would find Tom Riggles there before him. Miss Bessy Blunt was also present; and it was plain, from the expression of her speaking countenance, that she had not forgiven Ben, but tolerated him under protest. Our hero and sweet Nelly Blyth were not of the party, however, because they happened just then to prefer a quiet chat in the summer-house in the back-garden. We will not presume to detail much of the conversation that passed between them. One or two of the concluding sentences must suffice.

"Yes, Bill," said Nelly, in reply to something that her companion had whispered in her ear, "you know well enough that I am glad to-morrow is our wedding-day. I have told you so already, fifty times at least."

"Only thrice, Nell, if so often," said Bill. "Well, that *was* the luckiest shot the Frenchmen ever fired at me; for if I hadn't had my thumb took off I couldn't have left the sarvice, d'ye see; and that would have delayed my marriage with you, Nell. But now, as the old song says—

"No more I'll roam
Away from home,
Across the stormy sea.
I'll anchor here,
My Nelly dear,
And live for love and thee."

Other books by this author

Black Ivory

Red Rooney

The Coral Island

The Golden Dream

The Hot Swamp

The Island Queen

The Red Eric

Fast in the Ice

Sunk at Sea

Chasing The Sun

The Lively Poll

Choose from Thousands of 1stWorldLibrary Classics By

A. M. Barnard	Booth Tarkington	Edward Everett Hale
Ada Leverson	Boyd Cable	Edward J. O'Biren
Adolphus William Ward	Bram Stoker	Edward S. Ellis
Aesop	C. Collodi	Edwin L. Arnold
Agatha Christie	C. E. Orr	Eleanor Atkins
Alexander Aaronsohn	C. M. Ingleby	Eleanor Hallowell Abbott
Alexander Kielland	Carolyn Wells	Eliot Gregory
Alexandre Dumas	Catherine Parr Traill	Elizabeth Gaskell
Alfred Gatty	Charles A. Eastman	Elizabeth McCracken
Alfred Ollivant	Charles Amory Beach	Elizabeth Von Arnim
Alice Duer Miller	Charles Dickens	Ellem Key
Alice Turner Curtis	Charles Dudley Warner	Emerson Hough
Alice Dunbar	Charles Farrar Browne	Emilie F. Carlen
Allen Chapman	Charles Ives	Emily Bronte
Alleyne Ireland	Charles Kingsley	Emily Dickinson
Ambrose Bierce	Charles Klein	Enid Bagnold
Amelia E. Barr	Charles Hanson Towne	Enilor Macartney Lane
Amory H. Bradford	Charles Lathrop Pack	Erasmus W. Jones
Andrew Lang	Charles Romyn Dake	Ernie Howard Pie
Andrew McFarland Davis	Charles Whibley	Ethel May Dell
Andy Adams	Charles Willing Beale	Ethel Turner
Angela Brazil	Charlotte M. Braeme	Ethel Watts Mumford
Anna Alice Chapin	Charlotte M. Yonge	Eugene Sue
Anna Sewell	Charlotte Perkins Stetson	Eugenie Foa
Annie Besant	Clair W. Hayes	Eugene Wood
Annie Hamilton Donnell	Clarence Day Jr.	Eustace Hale Ball
Annie Payson Call	Clarence E. Mulford	Evelyn Everett-green
Annie Roe Carr	Clemence Housman	Everard Cotes
Annonaymous	Confucius	F. H. Cheley
Anton Chekhov	Coningsby Dawson	F. J. Cross
Archibald Lee Fletcher	Cornelis DeWitt Wilcox	F. Marion Crawford
Arnold Bennett	Cyril Burleigh	Fannie E. Newberry
Arthur C. Benson	D. H. Lawrence	Federick Austin Ogg
Arthur Conan Doyle	Daniel Defoe	Ferdinand Ossendowski
Arthur M. Winfield	David Garnett	Fergus Hume
Arthur Ransome	Dinah Craik	Florence A. Kilpatrick
Arthur Schnitzler	Don Carlos Janes	Fremont B. Deering
Arthur Train	Donald Keyhoe	Francis Bacon
Atticus	Dorothy Kilner	Francis Darwin
B.H. Baden-Powell	Dougan Clark	Frances Hodgson Burnett
B. M. Bower	Douglas Fairbanks	Frances Parkinson Keyes
B. C. Chatterjee	E. Nesbit	Frank Gee Patchin
Baroness Emmuska Orczy	E. P. Roe	Frank Harris
Baroness Orczy	E. Phillips Oppenheim	Frank Jewett Mather
Basil King	E. S. Brooks	Frank L. Packard
Bayard Taylor	Earl Barnes	Frank V. Webster
Ben Macomber	Edgar Rice Burroughs	Frederic Stewart Isham
Bertha Muzzy Bower	Edith Van Dyne	Frederick Trevor Hill
Bjornstjerne Bjornson	Edith Wharton	Frederick Winslow Taylor

Friedrich Kerst	Hayden Carruth	James Branch Cabell
Friedrich Nietzsche	Helent Hunt Jackson	James DeMille
Fyodor Dostoyevsky	Helen Nicolay	James Joyce
G.A. Henty	Hendrik Conscience	James Lane Allen
G.K. Chesterton	Hendy David Thoreau	James Lane Allen
Gabrielle E. Jackson	Henri Barbusse	James Oliver Curwood
Garrett P. Serviss	Henrik Ibsen	James Oppenheim
Gaston Leroux	Henry Adams	James Otis
George A. Warren	Henry Ford	James R. Driscoll
George Ade	Henry Frost	Jane Abbott
Geroge Bernard Shaw	Henry James	Jane Austen
George Cary Eggleston	Henry Jones Ford	Jane L. Stewart
George Durston	Henry Seton Merriman	Janet Aldridge
George Ebers	Henry W Longfellow	Jens Peter Jacobsen
George Eliot	Herbert A. Giles	Jerome K. Jerome
George Gissing	Herbert Carter	Jessie Graham Flower
George MacDonald	Herbert N. Casson	John Buchan
George Meredith	Herman Hesse	John Burroughs
George Orwell	Hildegard G. Frey	John Cournos
George Sylvester Viereck	Homer	John F. Kennedy
George Tucker	Honore De Balzac	John Gay
George W. Cable	Horace B. Day	John Glasworthy
George Wharton James	Horace Walpole	John Habberton
Gertrude Atherton	Horatio Alger Jr.	John Joy Bell
Gordon Casserly	Howard Pyle	John Kendrick Bangs
Grace E. King	Howard R. Garis	John Milton
Grace Gallatin	Hugh Lofting	John Philip Sousa
Grace Greenwood	Hugh Walpole	John Taintor Foote
Grant Allen	Humphry Ward	Jonas Lauritz Idemil Lie
Guillermo A. Sherwell	Ian Maclaren	Jonathan Swift
Gulielma Zollinger	Inez Haynes Gillmore	Joseph A. Altsheler
Gustav Flaubert	Irving Bacheller	Joseph Carey
H. A. Cody	Isabel Cecilia Williams	Joseph Conrad
H. B. Irving	Isabel Hornibrook	Joseph E. Badger Jr
H. C. Bailey	Israel Abrahams	Joseph Hergesheimer
H. G. Wells	Ivan Turgenev	Joseph Jacobs
H. H. Munro	J. G.Austin	Jules Vernes
H. Irving Hancock	J. Henri Fabre	Julian Hawthrone
H. R. Naylor	J. M. Barrie	Julie A Lippmann
H. Rider Haggard	J. M. Walsh	Justin Huntly McCarthy
H. W. C. Davis	J. Macdonald Oxley	Kakuzo Okakura
Haldeman Julius	J. R. Miller	Karle Wilson Baker
Hall Caine	J. S. Fletcher	Kate Chopin
Hamilton Wright Mabie	J. S. Knowles	Kenneth Grahame
Hans Christian Andersen	J. Storer Clouston	Kenneth McGaffey
Harold Avery	J. W. Duffield	Kate Langley Bosher
Harold McGrath	Jack London	Kate Langley Bosher
Harriet Beecher Stowe	Jacob Abbott	Katherine Cecil Thurston
Harry Castlemon	James Allen	Katherine Stokes
Harry Coghill	James Andrews	L. A. Abbot
Harry Houidini	James Baldwin	L. T. Meade

L. Frank Baum
Latta Griswold
Laura Dent Crane
Laura Lee Hope
Laurence Housman
Lawrence Beasley
Leo Tolstoy
Leonid Andreyev
Lewis Carroll
Lewis Sperry Chafer
Lilian Bell
Lloyd Osbourne
Louis Hughes
Louis Joseph Vance
Louis Tracy
Louisa May Alcott
Lucy Fitch Perkins
Lucy Maud Montgomery
Luther Benson
Lydia Miller Middleton
Lyndon Orr
M. Corvus
M. H. Adams
Margaret E. Sangster
Margret Howth
Margaret Vandercook
Margaret W. Hungerford
Margret Penrose
Maria Edgeworth
Maria Thompson Daviess
Mariano Azuela
Marion Polk Angellotti
Mark Overton
Mark Twain
Mary Austin
Mary Catherine Crowley
Mary Cole
Mary Hastings Bradley
Mary Roberts Rinehart
Mary Rowlandson
M. Wollstonecraft Shelley
Maud Lindsay
Max Beerbohm
Myra Kelly
Nathaniel Hawthrone
Nicolo Machiavelli
O. F. Walton
Oscar Wilde
Owen Johnson
P.G. Wodehouse
Paul and Mabel Thorne

Paul G. Tomlinson
Paul Severing
Percy Brebner
Percy Keese Fitzhugh
Peter B. Kyne
Plato
Quincy Allen
R. Derby Holmes
R. L. Stevenson
R. S. Ball
Rabindranath Tagore
Rahul Alvares
Ralph Bonehill
Ralph Henry Barbour
Ralph Victor
Ralph Waldo Emmerson
Rene Descartes
Ray Cummings
Rex Beach
Rex E. Beach
Richard Harding Davis
Richard Jefferies
Richard Le Gallienne
Robert Barr
Robert Frost
Robert Gordon Anderson
Robert L. Drake
Robert Lansing
Robert Lynd
Robert Michael Ballantyne
Robert W. Chambers
Rosa Nouchette Carey
Rudyard Kipling
Saint Augustine
Samuel B. Allison
Samuel Hopkins Adams
Sarah Bernhardt
Sarah C. Hallowell
Selma Lagerlof
Sherwood Anderson
Sigmund Freud
Standish O'Grady
Stanley Weyman
Stella Benson
Stella M. Francis
Stephen Crane
Stewart Edward White
Stijn Streuvels
Swami Abhedananda
Swami Parmananda
T. S. Ackland

T. S. Arthur
The Princess Der Ling
Thomas A. Janvier
Thomas A Kempis
Thomas Anderton
Thomas Bailey Aldrich
Thomas Bulfinch
Thomas De Quincey
Thomas Dixon
Thomas H. Huxley
Thomas Hardy
Thomas More
Thornton W. Burgess
U. S. Grant
Upton Sinclair
Valentine Williams
Various Authors
Vaughan Kester
Victor Appleton
Victor G. Durham
Victoria Cross
Virginia Woolf
Wadsworth Camp
Walter Camp
Walter Scott
Washington Irving
Wilbur Lawton
Wilkie Collins
Willa Cather
Willard F. Baker
William Dean Howells
William le Queux
W. Makepeace Thackeray
William W. Walter
William Shakespeare
Winston Churchill
Yei Theodora Ozaki
Yogi Ramacharaka
Young E. Allison
Zane Grey